Secrets of Inner Power

BY ROY EUGENE DAVIS

Time, Space and Circumstance

SECRETS OF
INNER POWER

By

ROY EUGENE DAVIS

FREDERICK FELL INC.   **NEW YORK**

For information address:
Frederick Fell, Inc.
386 Park Avenue South
New York 16, N.Y.

Library of Congress Catalog Card No. 64-17301

Published simultaneously in Canada by
George J. McLeod, Limited, Toronto

Manufactured in the United States of America

CONTENTS

Secrets of Inner Power

1

YOUR PERSONAL FORMULA
FOR SUCCESS

It has been said that man can be anything, do anything and have anything in this world—if he can first believe it possible of attainment. Do you believe this? If you do, then the rest is easy. If you can step out in the direction of your dream fulfilled, with the conviction in your breast that it is already as good as established, you will meet with success not known to those of lesser vision.

A standard reference work* gives us this definition of success: "The favorable termination of a venture." How many people do you know who are successful in every area of their life pattern? How many actually accomplish that which they set out to accomplish?

Most of us succeed part of the time but statistics reveal that only 5 percent of the men and women in this country

* *Webster's New Collegiate Dictionary.*

9

are successful. The other 95 percent of the people flounder about as best they can. Not because they don't desire anything better from life, but because they haven't learned how to attune themselves to the basic laws of successful living.

It's up to you. By following basic, never-changing laws, you can put order into your present life pattern; or, if you would like to turn your attention to the accumulation and management of wealth, you can do that too. What has been done by one person can be done by another . . . by you, for instance. And, the bold assertion that it will be done is the first step in the right direction.

The second step is to do your best to move into a proper relationship with the laws of successful living. You can do this by reading books of an inspirational nature and by associating with people who are doing the things you want to do in life. When you do this, you learn to see life from their point of view and you can then operate as they do, but in your own life pattern, of course. You can do anything you feel you can do. Once, during a lecture that I was giving, on a subject that ties in with this theme, a lady in the audience spoke up and said, "What you are talking about reminds me of what a friend in Texas once told me. This friend said, 'Down here in Texas, a man can do anything he's big enough to do.' " You might remember that thought because it puts it in a nutshell. You can do anything you are big enough to do. If you cannot seem to do the things you feel inspired to do, then do some work on the inner man and make him larger.

The philosophers from the Orient are fond of telling stories that leave an impact on the listener. One story they tell is of a man who was lost in a hot, dry climate. After several miserable hours of wandering about in the burning sun, this man came to the edge of a small lake. Thankful that it wasn't a mirage, he dropped to his knees and bent over to take long, thirsty swallows of the water. In his urgency he felt as though he could drink the lake dry but found before long that he could only hold a volume of water equal to his capacity. Now many people are like this in relationship to the blessings of life, which exist in quantity and quality, waiting to be taken. They feel that they want to live in a world of abundance . . . they want to have plenty of money with which to buy the objects of their desire . . . they want companionship . . . they want to experience good health . . . they want to have spiritual insight. But, alas—they are limited in their capacity to receive and hold, that which is ever available. They can only possess that which they can feel natural in handling. This book is designed to show you how to handle success.

Conception precedes birth. The mind of man must first conceive of an event as being possible before the event can be experienced as a reality. By reality, I mean that it must be real to the sense of sight, the sense of touch, the sense of smell, and so on. It must be real to your three-dimensional perception.

Most people are running on subconscious conditionings or recordings. They do not really think at all. They move through life mumbling such phrases as, "It can't happen to me . . . it's too good to be true . . . good fortune can't last." And, since this is the thinking and feeling, this is what manifests itself in the life experience.

You must learn to reverse the gears of your mental machinery and begin to say, "I can move ahead . . . I will do something about my life," and then go ahead and do it. Nothing can take the place of action motivated from an inner conviction of certainty. Nothing can stand in the way of the will, drenched with flaming conviction that the deed is as good as done and the goal as good as attained.

Here is a key to remember:

Your dominating thoughts mold and shape your consciousness and your state of consciousness determines your lot in life.

Your dominating thoughts, those thoughts which you allow to percolate through the subconscious during all of your waking moments, continue to work even when you are not awake, and they gradually but surely shape your outlook on life and, hence, your destiny. Ralph Waldo Emerson, with his remarkable knack of cutting through surface clutter, had this to say: "A man is what he thinks about all day long." You are what you think and feel. Your train of thoughts issue forth in keeping with your level of awareness, which is another way of referring to your state of consciousness.

Naturally, you want to be free and creative, and you will see right away how important it is to control your thoughts and feelings. You may think that this is beyond you when you first begin to take command. The habit of letting things slide is a strong one, but you can break it if you really want to. You can take command of your thoughts and feelings by making a conscious attempt to control your speech. When you speak with conscious conviction, you automatically take command of your thought stream. It is not so much a matter of effort as it is a matter of directed attention. Or, consider it a matter of flowing your attention. The easier you expect it to be, the easier it will be.

Practice, from this moment on, speaking only those things you desire to be true for you. The rest of the time, if you are tempted to indulge in gossip and negative discussions, maintain a noble silence. A little "shop talk" now and then is all right, of course, but steer clear of long meaningless sessions which only tend to confirm your fears and frustrations. You needn't be a pious or holier-than-thou type, but do have a direction and a purpose in life. This will give you control of your thoughts and feelings. It will magnetize you and give you an aura of power.

When you write letters to friends, make them sparkle with life and confidence. Check the impulse to ramble on and on about the small, unpleasant things in your environment. Be an optimist and really feel it.

I'm not talking about false enthusiasm which leaves you drained and empty, but I am suggesting that you find a new depth to give your life stability. When I lecture I try to get right to the point and let the facts speak for themselves. A friend of mine once attended a sales seminar conducted by a real live-wire speaker. This friend told me later, "Roy, you ought to take a leaf from that man's book . . . why, he's so full of enthusiasm he jumps three feet off the floor to drive home a point. Boy, he is really a spellbinder!" I said, "What did he have to say?" My friend said, "Just the usual stuff and not too well organized at that, but boy, could he get you excited!" This speaker used enthusiasm to stir up the crowd to get them ready for the killing. When he got them to the right pitch he brought out his wares and sold a large percentage of the people in attendance. After he left town, many of these people felt that they had been used. Genuine enthusiasm, springing from belief in his product plus a zest for life would have resulted in just as good a meeting and results that would have lasted for a longer period of time.

Do not blame yourself for all of your negative thoughts and feelings. Many of your dominant thought patterns were "planted" in the soil of the subconscious without your knowledge. At times in your life, when you are relaxed and maybe feeling a bit under the weather, when you are passive, you are wide open to suggestion and you absorb any thought or idea that comes your way if it is directed with enough conviction. You are manipulated by your environment. A passive person is an advertising man's dream. He can be made to think anything. He can be taught to buy a certain product, fall in line with a party line and agree to even the weirdest of philosophies. The human mind is such that it likes to think like the masses because it feels more secure.

Children are taught to believe in a certain way . . . they are conditioned to agree to get along with society . . . to grow up, to marry, to work, to retire and eventually to move on and make room for others. Few people even examine why they do the things that they do. Fewer still have the nerve to break with these "race beliefs" of how a human being should operate. I feel that it is desirable to find the right place in this world and to know why things are as they are. One of the most satisfying experiences that anyone can have is to unravel the riddle of life. I consider the person who accomplishes this a very successful person indeed.

Break loose from the limiting concepts that hem you in. Remember—whatever you can conceive, you can experience. You live in a universe of inexhaustible substance. You can take it and form it as you will as long as you operate in line with the universal laws. In fact, you might even assume the viewpoint that you are an instrument of Universal Mind and that it is your responsibility to do what you can to bring about a better world order. You can work from where you are and follow your guidance from there . . . always in line with what is right, for you and for others with whom you come in contact.

Many men can trace their feelings of poverty to the

time when someone told them, with emotion, "You are no darn good, you never were and you never will be." Or, "You will never amount to anything in this world . . . you are shiftless, lazy, good for nothing." Common sense will say these accusations are not true; yet, when a person is on the receiving end of such a verbal barrage, especially if he has some respect for the person who is talking, he is very receptive and receives this inflow as though it were a hypnotic command. And, even though he knows better, when he is tired or experiences a temporary business reversal, he will tend to believe according to these commands.

There is no point in resenting people who steered you in the wrong direction along life's pathway; they may have thought they were doing you a favor, or they didn't realize the far-reaching effects of their emotional outburst. Impersonalize the origin and try to do your best to neutralize these patterns. One of the best ways to do this is to replace the negative feelings with positive feelings. Make a conscious effort to do this. In time, you will overcome your limitations. By doing your best to move in the right direction you will soon find yourself becoming a hopeless success. You won't be able to help yourself. If you are already successful you will become more so, or perhaps even branch out into new areas of creativity. There is no limit to what you can do when you open up.

Many men who have learned to operate with comparative freedom in this world, move in many fields of endeavor, on many levels. They are able to shift their attention from one line of thought to another, quickly and easily. They have mastered their environment. One such man is the radio and television star, Art Linkletter. Here is a man who is very much alive, and all who watch him on one of his many appearances are impressed by his quick mind and ability to handle himself. He is one of the many thousands who began with very few of this world's goods and today is a success. He has his money and attention tied up in over thirty different business enterprises. He has a great feeling for people and we all sense it. He is not afraid to get in tune with life, on all levels. And, this is important.

Maybe you are doing the best you can and yet you are not making the grade. Do you harbor such thoughts as, "A person can't be materially successful and spiritual at the same time"? This is an area of conflict in many men and women. Resolve this idea now by coming into the realization that Spirit is the substance of this world. There is only one substance, variously formed. Science bears this out. It isn't some vague metaphysical concept that is hard to understand. Also, realize that your body is geared to living in this world and in order to do it you must be in tune with the things of this world. It isn't a matter of being a materialist, for you know there is Intelligence and Order behind the scene. You simply must operate on this level because it is the only one you know. But, you can use the subtle laws in order to live a richer, fuller life.

We now know that the mind of man is much like a computer. For the most part it is "programmed" or conditioned to react in certain ways to life situations. You are not the mind but you use the mind as an instrument so you can express on this plane. You do not have to think to be . . . you can just be aware, but this is a matter for a later chapter.

If the data you have stored in the subconscious is composed of hearsay information and false concepts, when you draw it out and relate it to present situations, you will draw erroneous conclusions. Even if the mind works well, if the data are incorrect you will get the wrong answers. If the data are correct you will get correct answers. It is that simple. Do you see the importance of having correct data?

An ancient sage said this: "All of man's problems are due to the fact that he is ignorant of his real nature." Think about it. If you look at life from the viewpoint of being a limited, helpless creature of circumstance, you can readily understand why you have one series of problems after another. If, however, you move into the proper viewpoint, and assume a place which would imply that you are the master, why then you can do great things.

Whatever you are exposed to, you retain. You may not be able to remember it because most of us conveniently forget so as to avoid responsibility. But, you can remember everything, and at will, when you assume the responsibility for doing so. As you become more aware, the barriers between the layers of mind fade away. There is only one mind. The human mind is the individualization of Universal Mind. There are compartments in the mind. The level through which we view life on the conscious level is called the conscious mind. On this level we can observe, draw conclusions, relate the present with the past, make decisions, exercise the will, and so on. On the subconscious level we store our memories and reactive patterns. Here we instill habit patterns and hide our experiences of pain and failure and to the extent that we do this are we inhibited and tied up on the psychic level. Wherever we suppress a memory or a painful pattern, we cloud the awareness. Life is that much more difficult for us because the awareness that we ought to have is dimmed. Given enough of these clouded areas, man grows old, gives up and dies. This is the cause of death, from the metaphysical point of view. As we go through life we accumulate a load of psychic injury and it eventually causes us to fade from the scene.

Your fondest dreams can be "believed" into existence —often, in ways that you could not imagine as being possible. Here is a story of one man's dream and how it came into being on this plane:

Many years ago, a young man in Los Angeles, California, read a book by the famed teacher of mental science, Judge Thomas Troward. This young man was impressed by the book and resolved that he would one day teach this science. He took the first step, according to his best judgment, rented an office and put out an advertisement. During the first six months he received only one student, and after being instructed for a while this student left with the decision that the young man was hopeless and didn't know what he was talking about.

It was obvious to him that this was not the way to take the message to the world . . . and besides, he was beginning to believe that the world didn't want it. So he took another job. One day, an associate happened to notice the book on the young man's desk and asked if he could read it. Permission was given and he took it home. In a few days he returned and asked if a meeting might not be held at his home so that a few of his friends could sample the teachings. It was arranged . . . and inside of two years, this young man, whose name was Ernest Holmes, was speaking to thousands of men and women in the Los Angeles area. He knew what he wanted to do, he believed in it, and it worked out. Today Ernest Holmes' students number in the hundreds of thousands. Large theaters are filled to capacity every Sunday in West Coast cities, where capable lecturers teach the Science of Mind as outlined by Dr. Holmes. A few years ago, a million-dollar temple was dedicated as the headquarters and a nine-story office building was being planned to house the administrative activity. Yes, we can believe our dreams into manifestation.

You see, Universal Substance wants to form, this is the nature of Substance, but it must have a pattern about which to form . . . and you supply that pattern when you maintain the image in your mind of what you want to experience in this world.

Now, let me touch upon the superconscious faculty, that layer of mind transcending subconscious and conscious layers. The superconscious area, being unclouded, is able to act as a transparent medium for Truth. Here, we are able to operate intuitively. We get the facts of life right from the storehouse of all knowledge. Through this layer streams the inspiration of genius and creative ability. We can all learn to be open to this area of pure knowledge if we will confront it.

Of course, it may be only a matter of definition, but I feel that many writers really refer to the superconscious level when mentioning the subconscious in terms of that layer of mind which is creative. The subconscious only receives impressions and reacts accordingly, without thinking. It is the superconscious awareness filtering through on the conscious and subconscious level that makes the difference.

Intuitively, we all know that what really matters in this world is our ability to produce the goods . . . to perform action where action counts, so . . . let's get down to business. For the next few weeks, spend your time in doing only those things that have a direct bearing on your goals. This can be the difference between mediocrity and outstanding success. Be sure not to waste your time, and, on the other hand, do not let others waste your time either. You may have to discipline yourself but you can do it if you are serious about it.

Map out a plan of action for the next month—for the next three months . . . for the next six months. Do it right now while it is on your mind. Write it out in detail on a plain sheet of paper. Think it through, then put it down in black and white where you can see it. Ask yourself, "What do I really want to accomplish in life?" Then, get the feeling of when you would like it to take form. Nail it down in time. What can you do now to get the project started?

Before you go any further with this book, get your paper and write these things out and don't be afraid to use your imagination.

When you contemplate the future, get the feeling of the picture being complete. Leap over the distance of time and space, in your mind's eye, and from desire to the feeling of accomplishment. When you write these things down, get the feeling that they are real, sense them to be here and now.

Do not show your outline to anyone. There is nothing mysterious about this suggestion. You can, of course, share your dreams with another person who is interested in the same things and if your efforts are to be joined. However, if you are working alone, keep things to yourself for if you show your outline to someone who does not share your vision he might tend to discourage you and try to dampen your enthusiasm. Unsuccessful people sometimes resent anyone who is making good. The only other person I would share my dreams with would be someone who, though not involved with me, would be able to see things from another point of view and might be able to give constructive suggestions.

This basic law of life: Desire fulfills itself, will be for you the key to the wonders of the world. Once you move into the level where you can begin to feel that your goals are almost ready to manifest, you will see opportunity at every hand to confirm your vision. This will give you faith and strengthen your resolve to live a creative life. Opportunity is all about us but we cannot see it if our mental attitude is negative and gloomy. When you alter your attitude you see a different picture altogether. Things may not change, but you see them in a new light.

Do not waste your time in talking too much about what you are going to do . . . just do it and then delight in the accomplishment. Some years ago, before I had really done anything in the writing field, I was talking with a man who had authored over forty books. Catching the vision of what I could do, I said, "Let me tell you what I'm going to do." He shot back, "Don't tell me, show me." It hit me right between the eyes and I resolved to get into action. Since then I have produced more than six books and booklets and dozens of magazine articles and . . . this is only the beginning.

I can hear you say now, "Yes, this all sounds well and good, but how do I get the feeling?" You want to move out in the direction of your dream but you don't know how to take that first step. You lack motivation. Then, read helpful books about men who are doing what you want to do. This will give you the picture and you can then identify with the picture. Go to the library and get books that will supply you with the information you need. Go to lectures that will inspire and motivate you. Get on the mailing list of book publishers and receive their regular notices of self-help books. It is our nature to identify with the object of our contemplation so when we contemplate the life pattern of others who are successful, we tend to identify with success.

When I read a book about a person who is doing the things I like to do, or would like to do, I put myself in that person's place. I see life from his point of view. Doing this, I can see how he thinks and feels . . . then I, too, can do what he is doing. Your environment is the reflection of your mental attitude. If you want to change it you must change yourself. You can solve any problem if you will shift your point of view from the concept of being problem-centered to the recognition of being problem-free. Remember what we said earlier? You can do anything you are big enough to do. Make yourself bigger than your problem and take dominion . . . and do it now.

For the most part, you will have to work from where you are until you get the feel of what I am talking about. Remember, you experience as you do because you are what you are. All experiences issue forth from your level of understanding. You are where you belong because of the concept you entertain of yourself. Sit quietly and think about this, regardless of your place in life. You are where you are because of a concept that you have which enables you to accept your present lot in life. If you are a multi-millionaire, a wage earner, or even if you are deep in the mire of poverty . . . you are where you are because of the concept that you entertain concerning your place in life. Now, it is quite easy to accuse others of being responsible for your situation, especially if you are not too well situated, but this will not alter things. The only thing that will alter your lot in life is your new mental picture, which you set in place, which defines just what it is you do want to experience. Man moves forward into his psychological assumptions.

Regardless of where you are in life, if you accept the basic principle that I have set forth here, you will begin to take control of your life pattern. It places you in the driver's seat. Instead of being acted upon by outside influences, you now realize that experiences meet you at your level of acceptance. So, you have been the master all along but you have been accepting limitation perhaps, or unhappiness, or frustration.

Do not lose sight of your true potential by wallowing in regret or feelings of guilt. Do not blame others and make them the object of your hate. No one ever did anything to you. People are instruments of Universal Mind and our life experiences come through them and meet us where we are, in understanding. Start now to move out with confidence and see what a joy it is to really live. Put some order into your environment. This will cheer you up and confirm the new decision that you have made. Discard the nonessentials and get down to the meat of the thing. Be fair and honest with yourself, for without self-honesty you will not have true success. If you deceive yourself you live blindly.

If you want to get anywhere you have to have a destination and a direction in which to move. This gives you a sense of stability and a reason for putting forth your creative energies. It enables you to see definite accomplishment of goals, each step adding to the realization of the "success-feeling" of previous accomplishments. It gives you a feeling of fulfillment and acts as a steady base from which to operate as you receive new inspiration to launch out into greater fields of endeavor.

You will be much happier if you are doing something that gives you a sense of purpose and when you know that others who are related to your life pattern are also benefited and uplifted. When you plan any enterprise you should plan it so that all who are a part of the plan will be uplifted, including yourself. Do not sacrifice yourself on the altar of service to others. This is an indication of a martyr complex. Serve yourself as well as others and in this way you will lift the over-all consciousness of the human race. We are not in this world alone. We must work in harmony with the larger plan if we are to be really successful. We ought not to try to become successful at the expense of another person. We do not have to use people and prey on them to secure our place in life.

A salesman ought to handle a product he really believes in and then he will be able to throw himself into his work. He is no longer selling a product; he is providing a service. When you provide a service you contribute to the over-all plan. I know of many salesmen who are stuck with a "gimmick" product and a "canned" sales talk. Their only incentive is a larger commission. They leave behind them a trail of unsatisfied customers and they soon become aware of this and wind up frustrated and cheated because of it. Do not bind yourself to a purposeless existence. Be creative.

Because I am a philosopher I believe we live forever, on some plane or another. With this perspective, how long will you continue in your present pattern? One year? Five years? Ten years? If you must alter your life sometime, why not now? What is the difference between your life situation now and what it will be several years from now? It will be different only as your point of view changes. Time, not being what we suppose it to be, has no power to alter our affairs. We do not have to wait for a period of time to change our viewpoint. We can do it sooner than we think if we will try. We cannot drift forever in a no man's land of indecision. The law of life is increase, expansion, greater expression. We can attune ourselves to this law and go along with it.

You have perhaps heard of "success techniques" that emphasized will power, struggle, strain, effort and the idea of "beating the other fellow to the punch." Or, perhaps the idea of finding the other fellow's weakness and taking advantage of it. I am constantly receiving circulars in the mail which describe books and courses based on the idea of making people do what you want them to do. Now, I realize, as do we all, that communication with people is important because people are instruments for the expression of life as it flows into form in this world. But, the idea of manipulating people for personal gain is offensive to me because

it is not the working out of the life plan, through the willing agents of the plan.

If you are a vibrant individual, you can sell anyone
almost anything but it does not mean that you have rendered them a service. In fact, if they have any influence and
speak to their friends about how they were duped into buying from you, it will hurt your business. If, however, you
open your mind to inner guidance and try to seek out the
people who want your product and who have the money to
pay for it and you work on this level, with a product that
is a real service, everyone is happy. You have been a bless-
ing to your fellow man.

In your dealings with members of your family, members of your church or community, if you try to really
communicate with them and really let life work itself out,
you will experience great harmony and peace of mind. I
know of many lives that have been in a constant state of
turmoil because of someone's urge to control another. Instead of trying to control another person, try getting into
communication with him and see if this will resolve the
problem. When you communicate with your environment
you find happiness. The next time you feel down in the
dumps and think the world is against you, do this: just
relax and gaze about yourself. See the area about you in
vivid detail. Feel the floor beneath your feet, the tempera-
ture and atmosphere of the room, the presence of other
people about you. Just relax and accept all of this and see
how wonderfully real it is. As you do this you will feel
your spirits rise. Why is this? Because you are communicating with your environment and perfect communication
resolves all problems. When you avoid certain areas of
responsibility, certain situations, feelings, you lose contact
with life at those points and this breeds emptiness.

Properly understood, it shouldn't be difficult to succeed in life. Whoever you are, wherever you are, you can find fulfillment doing what you feel led to do. As you practice it will become as natural as breathing . . . it will be automatic. Do not concentrate on the idea of overcoming obstacles; come to the point where you see the perfect expression of life acting upon itself in wonderful harmony and you are a part of this. See it all as an activity in mind. See yourself as an open channel for the flow of life on all levels. You might want to remember instances of how you felt when you experienced a smooth working out of situations in the past. You might want to run through portions of scripture or snatches of inspirational poetry. Anything to keep you in tune with life. Such affirmations, deeply felt, as: "I am an open channel through which the currents of Life are now flowing. This is my life, my health, my supply, my prosperity." The idea isn't to hypnotize yourself into believing it, but to bring yourself to the point where you recognize it to be true! This is not autosuggestion, it is self-realization! There is all the difference in the world. One is a conditioning process and the other is a process of release. One binds, the other liberates.

Many people are socially conditioned to feel guilty if they are not always tired and overworked, as if they had to experience this to justify their existence. It is a grave mistake to assume that physical exertion equals success. I'm not saying that we shouldn't be active, but we must get over the idea of earning our living by the sweat of our brow. There are thousands who work long hours and they just manage to get by. There are others who work on different levels, the realms of mind, and they realize vast returns for the time and energy expended.

There is a great difference between creative enterprise and just plain hard work. Learn to recondition yourself so that you begin to accept the possibility that you can have command over more of the things of this world. Enlarge your vision, learn to increase your capacity to receive. In the midst of so-called bad times, there are men and women who succeed wonderfully well. They do not concentrate on the over-all negative mental tone; they attune themselves to a different level of operation and they manifest success and prosperity. When you understand these principles you will never again allow trends, times and circumstances to hinder your free expression.

Time does not change anything, because it has no power to motivate. Our concept of time is a psychological thing . . . it is not an entity. We can move in consciousness and, for the most part, slip by the time factor. I mention this idea, for. the most part, because we deal with people who are anchored in a concept of time and we tend to take on part of their belief about it. Looking back over my life I can see where I could have accomplished more things or perhaps the same things at an earlier date if I had had the ability to see opportunity and the nerve to make my move when I had the urge.

A man may have all the talent and all the natural ability needed to succeed in his chosen area but lack confidence to make his move. In the words of Shakespeare, "There is a tide in the affairs of men which, taken at the flood, leads on to fortune." While lecturing in Miami one time I noticed a young man in the audience who seemed familiar to me. I knew I had seen his face somewhere. In the days that followed we had many pleasant conversations and I finally asked him if he had been in the public eye at any time. Then it clicked. He said he had a hit record a while before this and he told me how it came about.

He was in New York City and had written some songs, one of which, he felt, would be a hit if he could sing it and have a record made and promoted. He looked about him and saw many older men who had once cherished dreams of this nature, who had tried "to work their way up" but never arrived. While walking along Broadway at Times Square his eyes fell upon a billboard with a notice that it was for rent. He called the advertising agency and got the price of the space. Then he talked to his father, who was in the real estate business. When his father heard the idea he remarked, "It's just wild enough to go over."

Here was his idea, which he followed through. He conceived of a short note, to be displayed on the billboard, in full view of the many thousands that came through the Times Square area. The note began, "An open letter to Perry Como . . ." and went on from there. The direct approach worked and before long this young man had his record produced and he himself appeared on nation-wide television shows to promote it . . . and he had a hit. Later on, he decided to get out of this particular phase of the business. But he proved his point; he could do it if he wanted to and he didn't have to wait for time and circumstances to do for him what he could do for himself.

Some men work and struggle and attain a measure of success after many years of concentrated effort . . . whereas other men hit the top right away. Any man who succeeds in life deserves it because he has come to that point where he can accept it and that is the key to the whole thing. Success does not come as a reward for our efforts, however well intentioned they may have been, success comes as a result of our ability to take it.

Suggestions for Getting the Most from This Book

To get results you will have to apply yourself. You will have to put these principles into practice, for the experiences that stem from practice will confirm the validity of the principles.

Make it a plan to read over, this and all the chapters, at regular intervals. Pause to reflect a bit when you come to an idea or viewpoint that moves you. Allow it to sink in and register within you. Don't try to fight it intellectually but rather contemplate and reflect until the light dawns. Then, skim over the entire contents and let the main ideas sink into your subconscious and become a part of you. As you do this you will see things that you didn't notice before . . . because you have grown in stature and increased in awareness.

REMEMBER TO PRACTICE:

1. Remember what success means: "The favorable termination of a venture."
2. Believe that you can realize anything the mind can conceive.
3. Remember that "your dominating thoughts mold and shape your consciousness."
4. Get a clear understanding of the conscious, subconscious and superconscious layers of your mind.
5. Remind yourself, always "action where action counts" and "first things first."
6. Did you write your plans and goals in detail? Better check it over and get the FEELING of accomplishment.
7. Take dominion!
8. Your ability to succeed is in ratio to your capacity to accept, therefore enlarge your capacity.
9. Believe in yourself.

2

THE TECHNIQUE OF CREATIVE IMAGINATION

IMAGINATION ... the power that makes it possible for man to accomplish his heart's desire. Imagination has intrigued the greatest minds of the ages and it will continue to do so, for it holds the key to human destiny. The proper use of creative imagination when linked up with intuitive guidance gives man absolute mastery over his environment. We now know that people can, by exposing themselves to certain techniques and methodology, approach their true creative potential.

Just think of what this means! How much of your true potential are you using now? If you are the average person you are using only a fraction of it and you know it. Here, then, is a wonderful key that you can use to rise high in your chosen area of expression. Man is limited in life only by his lack of ability to use his imagination.

I am sure you will find, as have countless thousands before you, that as you practice in the realm of imagination, wonderful worlds of self-discovery will be revealed to you. Perhaps you are wondering if you can ever really experience an inner awakening . . . if you can ever know what it is like to be truly creative. Well, psychologists know that any primary ability can be trained, that even an average potential can be developed by exercise. I venture to say that as we progress in this chapter you will see how you have been using your imagination right along, although not always in the best manner.

Imagination Defined

Let us look at this word **imagination.** What does it mean? Often we are prone to use the term to mean something other than that with which we are presently dealing. For instance, we use the term in place of fancy or daydream. We say, when a person has had a flight of fancy, "Oh he—or she—is just imagining it." Because we do not always say what we mean and we do take liberty with words, the term **imagination** does not mean the same thing to all of us.

Let us begin with a common understanding of the term. *Webster's New Collegiate dictionary* gives this definition: *Imagination—The act or power of imagining; formation of mental images or objects not present to the senses, especially of those never perceived in their entirety; hence, mental synthesis of new ideas from elements experienced separately.*

Fancy is a term associated with gathering elements of a situation in the mind, but usually in a lighter vein and often as an escape from reality, rather than for the purpose of creating a new reality, closer to the individual desire. From what we now know, we may use the ability to fancy or assemble various elements of our inner world, but we must use imagination in order to bring it into reality. Fancy assembles, imagination creates.

Now follows the technique by which you will learn to move forward into your psychological assumptions and thus control your future experiences.

The Technique

First, retire to a quiet place where you will not be disturbed. Turn the lights low and make yourself as comfortable as possible. Loosen any articles of clothing that tend to restrict breathing or cause tension. Recline in a large, comfortable chair. Breathe deeply and relax and sink into a state of reverie . . . into the twilight zone . . . just between wakefulness and sleep. You are still alert and have control of the thoughts and feelings, but the tensions are gone and gone too are the cares of the moment. It is most important that you arrive at this in-between state, free of the pressures of the day.

Relax in a gentle sweep, from the top of the head down to the soles of the feet. Take a few deep breaths and let the air go with a sigh, releasing tension as you do. Just be quiet and rest in a neutral state of awareness . . . floating in time and space. Be at peace, with your eyes closed. This is not as difficult as it may sound, for we have all experienced this at one time or another. Just start to go to sleep but remain suspended halfway in the process.

The idea is to come to a point of awareness where you are still clear-headed but where you rest below the surface tensions and cares. The reason for this is so that when you use your creative vision you will not be restricted by conscious-mind fears and doubts. When you are resting in the twilight zone you have access to the fantastic worlds of the inner mind.

Use These Four Simple Steps

1. Relax and sink into the state of reverie as described above.

2. Create in your mind's eye a scene, a situation, a drama that would imply the fulfillment of your desire.

3. Get involved in this inner drama with feeling so that it becomes real to you. In fact, more real than anything you have ever known.

4. Go to sleep or sink deeper into your reverie state so as to seal the new experience within your being.

When you relax in the reverie state your mind is wide open to explore new and greater possibilities, without restrictions which ordinarily accompany the usual thought processes. For the time being you can roam in the vast worlds of imagination . . . where there are no limitations.

What Really Takes Place Within

When you create a scene that would imply the fulfillment of your dream or desire, you move it from the future to the present. You live in the situation, with feeling, as though it were true now . . . not as though it were going to be true. What happens when you do this? Since your subconscious does not know the difference between a real experience and an imagined one, if both are accompanied by the same feeling, when you select a situation in your reverie state and make it real by feeling, you begin to get the experience of what it would be like to have the experience in reality. The reason why you haven't been able to realize the fulfillment of your dream, whatever it might be, is that you have not been able to feel comfortable in the possession of it. When you get the practice of feeling that it is real, as you practice this technique, you will move steadily into the fulfillment of the dreams in this world. Because the psychological assumption of any desire automatically wills the fulfillment, because it lays down a living track of feeling over which you can pass.

We are dealing with one of the basic truths of life. Richard Roberts puts it this way, "There is at work in the world an influence which may be described as creative wherever it operates. It is capable of reinforcing life and enhancing natural faculty. For this there is impressive evidence."

While practicing the technique, you must get involved in the inner drama with intense feeling so that you know it to be real, otherwise it is merely an experience of daydreaming and a waste of time. Feeling makes it real to you.

Should you arise from your practice without sinking deeper into the reverie state you would lose some of the effect of your practice because you would find your new feeling canceled by conscious-mind evidence that might be to the contrary. You might come from your practice and confront evidence in your environment which by contrast is far removed from your inner envisioning and by contrast you would experience confusion. So follow your deep practice with a period of light sleep in order to establish the new feeling as a reality.

Now what takes place? With the new image established within you, you begin to see opportunities that before were overlooked. People, situations, ideas . . . all seem to flow to you because of your change in mental attitude. What happens between the time of the practice and the fulfillment of the dream is the result of successful practice. When you practice in this fashion you are working with basic causes . . . you are initiating action. You are opening your vision to the possibility of new experiences. Something seems to happen on the invisible level, perhaps because we do live in an ocean of mind-substance.

Making It Happen vs. Letting It Happen

We all know men and women who work hard, make the right contacts and live good lives . . . yet fail to accomplish anything. Why is this? Because they do not have the right outlook on life. They are still trying to make things happen instead of letting things happen. They are still trying to get instead of learning to give. The secret is to give up the existing concepts that keep us from seeing opportunity. This is not a form of mental magic . . . it is not a technique to make others do your will . . . it is only a method by which you can prepare yourself to accept the desirable things of life.

The most difficult part of this creative process is to wait with confidence while we see the opening in which we should move. We should check the tendency to force things to happen by putting the pressure on others. You will move into every desirable experience just as soon as you are able to synchronize your thoughts, feelings and actions in the right direction. If you are not moving ahead in life, ask yourself, "Am I following my inner guidance?" or, "If I moved into my dream, could I handle the responsibility?"

Use It Every Day

Henry J. Kaiser has been widely quoted for his philosophy of "imagineering." He has a great ability to imagine new and grand projects and then he follows through. In one interview he told of how he often lies in bed for a while in the morning, planning his day, getting pictures and plans formulated in his mind's eye. Often, he will get an insight into a new process or an interesting design and he will get into motion that very day to put it into effect . . . to make it a reality. He knows the value of imagination and he knows the importance of putting his dreams into the proper setting.

Even though we work from the abstract to the concrete, it all takes place in orderly fashion. We sometimes make the mistake of assuming that we have to get our fulfillment in some miraculous manner, although it seems to me that the effortless materialization of desires in step-by-step fashion is miracle enough, especially as everything works out in orderly sequence.

Technique the Same for Any Goal

Regardless of what you want to experience, the goal can be realized by the use of this technique. You may desire a home, you may desire companionship, you may desire social activity. Well then, follow the same basic rule. Relax in a quiet place, assemble in your mind's eye a scene that would imply the fulfillment of your dream. . . . See the people, talk to them, sense the atmosphere of the room or location, make it real. Have a wonderful time and then go to sleep.

When you get the feeling of accomplishment you will begin to do the things you need to do, if any, to bring it about. Until you get this feeling of accomplishment most of your actions will be waste motion because you will have no direction or purpose. But now you begin to move with confidence and in the right way . . . so it does spring from a deep sense of knowing within you.

You may examine yourself to see if you have any habit patterns or behavior patterns which tend to make you socially unacceptable. Then you will correct these things in your nature. Perhaps you will be motivated to read books, attend classes and do other things to round out your personality and make you strong and capable. You may learn to dress, walk, talk and act like the person you want to be. You will be reborn. You will learn to like people and you will begin to feel at home in this world.

I once talked with a young lady who told me that she had studied these principles for years under one teacher or another. She had a fine home and a good education but she wanted a husband. She claimed that she used all the methods to draw the right mate. She visualized and worked with creative imagination. When she met a nice young man she found that after two or three dates he would not call on her. The reasons? One was that she dressed in such a manner as to be superior to the man, and the second reason was that she had a speech impediment that could have been corrected with a little self-discipline but which was a cause of embarrassment to her escort when in a public place.

She was visualizing and hoping for the right man but she was also repelling the very thing she said she wanted because she would not take care of two minor details that were in her power to change. You see, we can work all we want on the mental level, but if we refuse to release things which stand between us and fulfillment, we must be content with a series of frustrating experiences.

Are you afraid, are you confused, are you uncertain? Then use this priceless key of creative imagination and move into the realm where you are confident, well-balanced and certain of yourself. As you practice being poised and confident you generate a kind of magnetism. You begin to radiate a charm that is compelling to others. They begin to want to be around you, to do things for you. We are attracted to others who are strong and confident.

Norman Vincent Peale has said that he has benefited from a little mental technique when he is confronted with a strange audience and has to warm them up to get his message over. He just stands on the platform for a few moments prior to a talk and looks over the crowd, and as he stands there he just "loves them." Then he talks, and the atmosphere is electric. The audience can feel him as he extends himself and reaches out to them and they react to it.

Advice to Wives

A housewife should picture her home life as being happy and desirable in every way. She should expect her children to be well and happy, to be obedient and orderly. She should expect her husband to be a good father and a good provider as well as an ideal mate. She should picture him in his right place so that he is happy and the activity in which he is engaged prospers. She should expect an adequate supply of money to flow into the home economy.

Many wives ruin their chance for happiness by browbeating their husbands. Instead of encouragement, the man of the house often gets only the nagging and verbal pummeling that forces him to perform his work as drudgery and takes the zest out of life. It is not right, nor is it fair for married couples to assume the attitude that they must deny themselves and make sacrifices to insure a happy home life. We are living in the twentieth century, not in pioneer days. We have many labor-saving devices available and we have the know-how that enables us to do more with what we have. Families ought to see to the security of their home, yes, but they also ought to live a little. They should enjoy life together.

In the light of our theme, it is wrong for a wife to demand that her husband be the sole source of her supply. Why shut off your flow of money and opportunity by saying that it must come through your husband? I am not advocating an outside alliance, but I am advocating a change in mental attitude. Think big, begin to see your blessings flowing into your life, get ideas, be enthusiastic. It may be that your husband will be inspired because of the new and vibrant mental atmosphere to expand and be more creative in his work. It may be that you will get ideas that will directly relate to his success. It may be that you will get an idea to write an article, enter a contest, begin to exercise some dormant talent. There is no limit to what you can do when you change your mind about life.

If you want something, such as a new coat, a new hat, that second car, a summer cottage, a vacation trip . . . and you have tried to talk your husband into it and failed, don't be bitter, don't nag. Be sweet and cooperative. Build a mental picture that would imply the fulfillment of your dream. Make sure it is in harmony with the plans of the rest of the family. That is, if your husband says that there isn't enough money at present to buy a new home and the lack of money seems to be the only drawback, then, before you visualize, get together as to where you would buy the home if you had the money. If your husband has his heart set on a country place, don't visualize a suburban dwelling and try to get things your way at his expense. Agree on the place and the style of home first, then "see" it as a finished reality. When you do this you are simply adding your creative power to bring the dream you both want into manifestation. To manipulate your life experiences at the expense of another person is not wise. It is a selfish attitude which can only breed unhappiness.

When you understand that life experiences are yours to the extent that you can picture and accept them, you will get over the feeling that you have to work the angles or get things by hook or by crook. Only believe and see the picture come into manifestation.

Often parents will have to deal with a child who seems hard to manage. Perhaps the child wets the bed or misbehaves in school or is argumentative. They wonder how to change the child when an appeal to reason does not seem to work. Often, the solution is not even to try to change the child, but to change the parents' mental attitude, because children respond to the psychic atmosphere in the home. Most parents know that their children are naturally telepathic. When a child is sleeping it can often be awakened simply by thinking about it. I know of homes where children never miss a meal, regardless of the time it is served, regardless of how far from the kitchen or dining room they may be sleeping. When others in the house begin to think of eating, the child wakes up. We should not look upon this as unnatural. On the contrary, it is the most natural thing in the world. Most people could be more aware than they are but they have suppressed this awareness.

Children reflect the parents' expectancy regarding their behavior and reaction. Often a mother or father will say, "But Susan doesn't know we have our little differences, we never talk in front of her." Or, "I always act calm and confident around the children but inwardly I worry so much about them." These inner feelings radiate and embrace the children even if the exterior pose is one of confidence and poise.

Parents should expect their children to get good marks

in school. They should picture them as being well and wholesome in their outlook on life. It may be that there are deeper problems that will have to be faced, but at least we make the task easier if we face them with optimism.

If you have a person in the home who is older and hard to live with (though I don't wish to imply that all older people are hard to live with), "expect" them to be harmonious and to find their place in the family pattern. If you have someone who is caught up with a drinking problem, "expect" them to be able to handle it and be more temperate. Do not crucify people with your negative thinking and believing. Release them and see them, in your mind's eye, as they can be.

When you look at life from this new viewpoint the world becomes new to you, a radiant, living thing. In truth, we are living in a sea of pulsating life. Here is what Sir James Jeans writes in *The Mysterious Universe:* "The stream of knowledge is heading towards a non-mechanical reality; the universe begins to look more like a great thought than like a great machine."

And Sir Arthur Stanley Eddington writes in *The Nature of the Physical World:* "In the world of physics we watch a shadowgraph performance of the drama of familiar life. The shadow of my elbow rests on the shadow table as the shadow ink flows over the shadow paper. It is all symbolic, and as a symbol the physicist leaves it. Then, along comes the alchemist Mind who transmutes the symbols. . . . To put the conclusion crudely, the stuff of the world is mind-stuff."

This world is not hard and unyielding as you have supposed it to be . . . it will bend to your will and flow before you as you take your mental stand. Few people take a stand and declare what they want in life . . . they just

take what comes to them as a result of their negative
thinking.

Two Strong Emotions That Control Your Life

There are two strong emotions that control our living
experience. They are faith and fear. Fear is really faith in
reverse . . . it is believing in what you don't want in your
life. Fear is limiting . . . it stifles initiative. It holds the
will in abeyance. It must be overcome.

The best way to cancel out a fear picture is to replace
it with a positive picture. The best way to avoid disaster
is to create success. You are what your believing is. Therefore, synchronize your feeling, thinking and action to make
your belief dynamic, then you will control your life
through faith. You will move out of the shadows and into
the light when you begin to live by faith, which is after all
a wonderful form of imagining . . . "for faith is the substance of things hoped for . . ."

So what kind of pictures are you planting in the soul
of your mind? Are you planting pictures of fear or pictures of faith? What kind of world are you building?
Which emotion dominates your life . . . faith or fear?

Say, "I Can" and "I Will"

This is what Ben Sweetland did and changed his life,
even after he had lived well into middle age. Ben Sweetland is a widely known consulting psychologist. His book,
I Can, has sold a million copies. Every few months I see
a new book of his being offered in the book stores. His instruction has been recorded for salesmen and prepared as
a course, and his books have been condensed and made into

long-playing records. There seems to be no end to this man's creative output. Yet it was not always like this.

Ben Sweetland knew of the laws of life, he read inspirational books and he was able to improve his way of life. But there was something more that he wanted. Then, he hit upon his magic formula. He began to see really what it was that made the difference between the average life and a truly inspired life. He didn't move out of his pattern of inertia right away, but he did begin to make his move in consciousness, where it counts.

Following that inward movement came the physical move . . . into a better home . . . into a more creative life pattern . . . into the place where he began to get more recognition for his work. He learned to break the stifling bonds of limitation, and by affirming "I Can and I Will" he was able to bless himself and, through this, hundreds of thousands of other men and women.

Many people really do not make use of their great talent until they get to the point where they are forced to do so. This is why I am a great believer in burning my bridges behind me. I believe in going all the way if I am going at all. Why live half a life? Why take half a chance and experience only partial success when by making and pressing your claim you can have the whole thing?

You Must Be Willing to Change

When you alter your thinking and believing you must be willing to change some of your ways if you are going to succeed. You must release the feelings and concepts that are holding you back. You must get rid of fear, of laziness, of complacency. You must embrace your new idea of life with boldness. You must have courage. Too many times we are afraid to be different, afraid to change, for fear of what others will think or say. Remember, it is your life and your experience.

The World as a Loose Garment

To handle the stuff of this world I am convinced that you have to be able to take it or leave it. Many people have so little confidence that they cling in desperation to what they have, for fear that if they lose it and strike out into the deep waters of life they will lose what they have and be left with nothing . . . even if what they have at the moment is very little. You must be the master, not the slave. To be the master you must move into the viewpoint where you can handle this world and the experiences in it. You must see it in the proper light and wear it as a loose garment. Remember, the world conforms to your belief in it, so everything in your world emanates from you.

Salesmen experience this when they begin to expect a summer slump in sales or when they begin to believe that a certain area is "dead" and a waste of time. They usually find what they are looking for. Remember always that "the world is the shadow of the mind."

Years ago, before I was known as a lecturer, I would sometimes go into a city with lots of good publicity and draw a very small audience. Another time I would go into a city with little or no publicity and do very well. I found that to the degree that I was able to persist in believing in myself and my place in life, did I see the results to confirm my expectations. But it was hard in the beginning to overcome the feeling of emptiness when the response was poor. Then a friend with much experience in this work told me, "If you can get the feeling that you are doing your best and that you are in your right place, eventually the

doors will open and everything will turn out all right."
I saw this to be true, as I was able to stay with it.

We must maintain our optimism even in the face of
failure in order to firmly set the picture of success in the
mind. If we give up we will never amount to anything. We
must persist when we feel we are right. What do others
know of the hours of inner turmoil that you go through as
you try to adjust to life? What can they know of your fear
and tremblings as you endeavor to fulfill your self in this
world? You must follow your own intuition and rise high
in your effort . . . and you will if you persist, even in the
face of adversity.

Everyone knows, for instance, of the great success
won by Lawrence Welk. He has been the butt of jokes for
years because of the type of music that he represents. In
his early career he was often hurt and disappointed by
people who criticized his manner of speaking and his style
of playing. But he didn't stop, he kept on, and today he
pleases and delights millions each week with his brand of
wholesome entertainment.

Too many men and women give up without a fight.
They should persist when they feel they are right, and the
tide will turn, for this is the law.

A Working Definition of Faith

When you have faith you frame your heart's desire as
a mental image and you sustain it. You do this until it
reflects in your environment as a reality. You simply sustain the positive mental picture, rejecting all evidence to
the contrary, until you see it come forth.

Faith works miracles. I have talked with young men
who have had experience in hitching a ride on the highway.
They tell me they are often able to get a ride merely by

"expecting" to get a ride. Many years ago when I had finished high school and decided to go to the West Coast, I unwisely spent my money before buying my ticket. Rather than accumulate enough for the trip by bus or train I decided to hitchhike. Although I was raised in Ohio, at this time I was in St. Petersburg, Florida. I got a ride as far as Pensacola, Florida, on the first day. The second morning was cold and a light rain was coming down. I stood by the highway with my characteristic pose, and in spite of my cheerful expression the cars just flew by as though I wasn't even there.

Gradually, as midmorning approached, the traffic became sparse and only now and then did a car come by. I decided to "set" my mental attitude. I knew a little about the idea by this time because I had read a number of books on Eastern thought and positive thinking. A few minutes after I had visualized a ride, a car went by at a pretty fast rate of speed and disappeared in the distance. All was quiet except for the gentle rain.

Glancing up the road in the direction the car had gone I saw what appeared to be the same car coming back. When it came even with me it made a U-turn and stopped. The door opened and a husband and wife, in a car already loaded with luggage, invited me to squeeze in with them. After we got on the road the wife said, "I don't know what made us do it, but after we passed you we both got the idea to turn back and pick you up. The strange thing is, we never pick up hitchhikers."

That one ride took me all the way to New Orleans. One ride for the whole day with people "who never picked up hitchhikers."

Take a businessman who wants to increase his sales and expand his service. Let him image himself as succeeding wonderfully well and he will immediately begin to re-

ceive a stream of impressions incidental to his business
and how it may be improved. He may also be inspired to
make new business contacts or add vitality to or drop
present contacts. He may get ideas on how to improve production, cut costs, reach more people, package his product
so it has more eye appeal or diversify his interests and expand into new markets. At any rate, it will begin with a
new concept of self and a new concept of his business. He
must make his move in consciousness first . . . he must prepare the way for the physical experience by opening the
psychological path.

Rejoice in the Good Fortune of Others

If you know of other people who are trying to get
ahead in life, wish them well. Help them along. See only
success for them. Do not fall into the trap of wishing them
ill with the idea that if they fail there will be that much
more for you. There is plenty of business for everyone, and
besides, there is another important reason why you should
wish your fellow man well.

There is a law of life that can best be stated in this
fashion: "I can only experience for myself that which I
can expect for another person." Remember, our experiences enter through the door of our belief. And, if we believe that another person can be sick, or can fail or make
mistakes . . . because we have this belief in our consciousness, it can also happen to us. Our negative thoughts do not
come back to us, they never leave as long as we maintain
them, and they modify our experiences and condition our
living pattern.

So, to succeed in life, wish the other fellow well. Rejoice in his happiness and success and the idea of success
and right action will become so much a part of you that

soon your whole beingness will be composed of it. Be willing to help others when you are prepared to help them. If you can give others a boost, do it. Do it out of your abundance. Be sure you know how to help before you get involved. Sometimes the best way to help is to leave people alone and let them unfold as best they can.

This is something you will have to decide with each instance. Just follow your intuition in each case rather than go by a fixed rule. Some people need help in a tangible way, such as financial backing, references, advice. Others need only your encouragement. Don't assume that because you made it the hard way that others must also do the same. Help people to help themselves.

Aim High, You Might as Well

Often we don't get anywhere with our projects because we fail to think in large terms. We think small, and there is no magic in small thinking. It has no power to inflame the imagination and stir the heart. To get things done you must aim high; reach for the stars. Even if you don't quite make it you will have gone farther than you would have traveled otherwise. You must extend yourself if you are to come into your full realization. You can do undreamed of things if you will only follow the faint stirrings of your heart . . . and aim high.

Besides, few people aim high, so there is plenty of room at the top. The bottom of the ladder is hopelessly overcrowded. Out of the thousands who strive, only a few attain. Why? Because man is afraid to think in large terms. He is afraid to aim high. You can be one of the few in life who think big and aim high and you can go over the top!

I may not be the best inspirational writer in the field

but I do not dwell on the negative side of the picture. I may not be the best speaker in the world but I cling to the belief that I will be heard. I know that a man is what he thinks he is, and so I aim high. Even when I appear to be doing well, I constantly visualize myself before vast audiences. I "feel" that my writings are reaching the millions of waiting hearts and minds. I am forever "imaging" my work in grand fashion. I do not believe this to be ego; I feel we owe it to ourselves and to our world, if we think we have something to offer, to offer it well and in quantity. The most important thing is not the personal recognition, for a person can only handle just so much of that; the important thing is that others who are on the borderline, who are looking for something to trigger off their faith, can be touched and inspired to make their move in life.

Resolve now to be the best in your field. If you are going to write, do it beautifully . . . if you are going to sing, sing like the angels . . . if you are going to teach school, be the best teacher there ever was. It really does not matter what you do in life as long as you feel you are making a contribution and that you are in your right place.

Expectancy and Acceptance

When you practice the technique as outlined in the first part of this chapter, do it naturally. There will come a time when you will not need to practice the formal method of visualizing. You will simply catch the picture and it will work out. When your expectant attitude is balanced with your ability to accept the new experience, then you will have the result.

A good friend of mine, Richard Giller, whom I first met in Miami, Florida, told me the following story: He had

been a middleweight lifting champion of the United States
at one time and had set some records in his weight class.
When I met him he was an investment counselor and
had attended a few of my lectures on the creative use of the
mind. Of course Dick had been using these principles before he ever met me but we found it mutually stimulating
to meet and talk.

A year or so after we met he got the urge to enter
a lifting meet, just to try his hand and see if he was as
good as he used to be. He made a series of good lifts at
the meet, then decided to break his old record in the snatch
lift. This is the lift where the weight is taken from the
floor, overhead, in one clean motion. He took the weight
and missed it. Then, on his next try, he paused before the
weight, closed his eyes, and in his mind's eye saw himself
being congratulated by his friends just as though he had
made the lift. Then, he opened his eyes and bent down to
grasp the bar, set himself and pulled! He claims it was the
easiest lift of his career, and it set a new record!

How many athletes can tell similar stories? In lifting,
as in any game or form of competition, the mental attitude is the most important thing after the body has been
trained to peak efficiency. It is surprising to many how they
can improve their game of golf or bowling when they catch
the picture of how easy it can be. If you can picture it
done, the body will follow along to confirm the picture.
See yourself as a skilled performer in the drama of life.
You can be the ideal husband, wife, lover, teacher or whatever . . . if you will only believe it to be so for you.

A man may attract to himself any force in the universe if he will make himself a fit receptacle for it, establish contact with it, and arrange conditions so that its nature
compels it to flow to him.

REMEMBER TO PRACTICE:

1. Review the technique.
2. Understand the mechanics of it, that it is only a technique to enable you to adjust the mental attitude.
3. Follow through and make any changes in personality if you need to do so.
4. Control your expectations.
5. Maintain the proper mental image at all times.
6. Believe the best for others as well as for yourself.
7. Aim high.

3

AWAKENED IMAGINATION

Man is on the threshold of a new frontier! He is now breaking new trails in the mysterious regions of the mind. Imagination is the one ability that man has, that no other life form can use. Man can imagine how it would be to do new things and then follow through and do them. Animals are "programed" to follow their basic pattern, but man can move in the realm of ideas and then translate his ideas into the substance of this world.

The more we use the imaginative faculty, the more it awakens, the more proficient we become in its use and the more freedom we experience. I want to stress here that the technique of creative imagination is an awakening technique, not a conditioning technique. I know some readers will say, "This method seems like autosuggestion or self-hypnosis." It is quite possible that there is a similarity up to a point—that is, up to the point where reverie is experienced. But here, the methods differ. With auto-conditioning we try to record a belief on the subconscious layer of mind so that we henceforth operate from that conditioning. With the proper use of the technique of creative imagination we try to come to the point where we awaken to the realization that the truth about life we are affirming is real. One is a conditioning process, the other is an awakening process. When you awaken you are free.

Auto-conditioning techniques tend to continue the formation of patterns on the subconscious level. A person who is conditioned into a belief pattern is limited by that belief pattern. He reacts. He does not really see. He does not really respond to life with full awareness. His life is more mechanical.

I once met a man who had worked hard all of his life. He came into some money and made wise investments. He no longer had to go to work every day as he had done for so many years. He told me, "I feel out of place during the day until its five o'clock, then I can relax." This was his normal quitting time. His subconscious was conditioned to the idea of working a steady eight hours every day. He didn't feel comfortable when he changed his pattern, and gradually had to outgrow this feeling so that he could turn his attention to other, more important things.

Many children are taught to believe in a God who grants or withholds blessings. When they grow up they begin to realize that the blessings in life appear according to law, according to their own ability to remain in tune with the laws of right action. Yet, they still maintain this lingering subconscious belief of a man-God and this creates much inner conflict. A belief pattern may help an ignorant person stay on the straight and narrow path, but it will be troublesome to a person who is beginning to awaken.

The Fourth-Dimensional Viewpoint

All events and all possible human experiences exist now in time, as permanent realities. Somewhere, someone is now having the experience you claim you desire for yourself. Try to get the viewpoint that all feelings exist now . . . and you can move among them and accept them at will. As a large room can contain many chairs, set at different angles yet all accessible to you, so this thing called life contains many events which are all set and accessible to you . . . waiting for you to choose and make your claim.

When you awaken to this point you begin to see into the nature of things. You see that the only cause is in your own mind . . . everything else is the result of the mental decision. The initial intention is the most important factor. One may say that a ball bounces from the wall because it was thrown against the wall, thus citing an example of cause and effect. But the truth of the matter is that the whole operation is the result of the decision made in the mind of the thrower. The throwing and the rebounding is effect.

Too often we try to comprehend life from surface indications, without really seeing the causes which exist in the mind of man. All experiences have their origins in mind. Everything issues forth from mind. All that takes place in this world to make your dream a reality is the result of your state of consciousness, your concept of yourself, gained in the silent practice of creative imagination. Your world reflects your attitude, let there be no doubt about this.

When we learn to recognize that state of consciousness that we desire to be permanent within us, and live in it with feeling, then the mechanics take care of themselves. The human mind often gets confused with so much commotion in living and tries to read between the lines when, in truth, there may be nothing there. We must find the cause behind every experience and work from there.

When you decide to have a certain experience, and you establish this realization within, all you have to do then is wait and see it unfold. Stand still, in the full realization that your own will be presented to you, without force or strain, without a hardship being worked on anyone.

I heard the story of a man in California who taught practical psychology. He had always yearned for an island off the coast where he could establish a retreat for men and women who wanted to get away from it all for a while. He didn't have the resources but it didn't stop him from dreaming. One day he met a man and it turned out that this man bought an island and built the buildings and gave it to him. It cost over a quarter of a million dollars and the rich man gave it just as easily as the average person might serve a cup of coffee.

Another man I know was once a traveling lecturer. He got the idea that he would like to see some of his books in the public libraries. He picked the three best titles and took them to a printer to get a price on the printing of them. The estimate was for $10,000 for ten thousand books. He didn't do anything about it just then but he held to his original idea. One night, after a lecture, a man came forward to tell him how much he enjoyed his work, then asked if there was anything he might do to show his appreciation.

The lecturer said, "No, I have everything I need."

"But," the man insisted, "isn't there anything you want to do, any pet projects you have in mind?"

"Oh, I thought I might get a few books published and place them in libraries."

Whereupon the man pulled his checkbook from his

coat pocket, asked how much it would cost, and wrote a check for the full amount. He had the means and it was his pleasure to do it.

Make No Provision for Failure

When you start a project, from the very beginning act as though you cannot fail. Do not spend more money than you can command at the time, nor overextend yourself, but move right out with ambition as though you fully expect to carry your plans through to completion. Drive the failure fears from your mind. Get rid of them. Wipe them out by constantly affirming success and right action.

Get involved in your project. Tell only those people who are to be involved, for the time being. If you talk too much to people who have no real interest in you, they will tend to make fun of you and kid you if you don't make progress as fast as you think you should. Conserve your energies, direct your attention, get things done.

You Live More When You Control Your Attention

When you control your attention you put more living experience into a shorter time. And, it seems to be true that the more you do, the more alive you are, the more you can do. Increased awareness makes you that much more efficient. A sluggish person just manages to eke out an existence.

There is more to life than in just getting by. Learn to do what is necessary to get things done . . . then you will have energy to turn to some other worthwhile projects. You may have noticed, as I have, that many creative people are really quite adept in several lines of endeavor. They can handle more of life.

Take for instance W. Clement Stone of Chicago, who heads four insurance companies, publishes *Success Unlimited* magazine, and is responsible for the Napoleon Hill Institute. Besides this he lectures all over the country, has co-authored an inspirational book, and just as this chapter is being prepared I see by the newspaper that he is receiving an award for being the Christian Layman of the Year. The caption under the picture mentions his interest in the Boys Clubs of America.

Tom O'Neil of Southern Pines, North Carolina, has an all-night golf course, a fine restaurant, puts out an occasional record in which he is featured on the harmonica, and is also the publisher of the *Psychic Observer*, a newspaper catering to a large reading public with an interest in the higher powers of the mind.

A recent article in *Fortune*, describing the activities of business executives, points out that many of them have a restless urge to do many things. They must be doing things in order to be happy.

Dr. Preston Bradley, pastor of Chicago's Peoples Church, is a man of many talents. In one week his schedule ran like this: taped a biweekly television show and some of his fifteen weekly radio broadcasts, consulted his publisher about his ninth book (an autobiography), wrote an editorial and a sermon for his monthly magazine, spoke at half a dozen luncheons and dinners, attended civic committee meetings, conducted weddings, handled funerals, and visited the sick members of his congregation of four thousand. For fifty years he has been Chicago's leading voice of liberal Protestantism.

After a man reaches a certain point in the world where he knows he can command anything at all in life, he gets over the compulsive urge to accumulate money and property just for the doing of it, and, instead, begins to think in terms of channeling his wealth in the right way. Hugh Roy Cullen is a fine example of this. Mr. Cullen worked hard to find oil and, when he found it, began to divert the wealth into constructive channels. One time, in less than forty-eight hours, he gave more than four and a half million dollars to four different hospitals, with no strings attached to any of the gifts. Another time he had attorneys draw up papers to create a foundation in which oil properties estimated to produce thirty to forty million barrels of oil, worth eighty million dollars or more, would be channeled into the Texas Medical Center and the University of Houston.

Prosperous men do not always give because they are trying to make up for past ruthless methods. They often give because they have found that power makes them humble and with it comes increased responsibility.

David Murdock of Phoenix, Arizona, raised himself to a towering stature in the building business and is still going strong. He has a terrific ability to envision what he wants and even though he aims high (he thinks he will be worth over $100 million within the next ten years), he looks at life from the right mental attitude. He says, "I'm interested in creating things, for creativity is the life of the world. My buildings are making me rich, but they are making the city bigger, stronger, richer, too."

There is a chance that many people reading this book will look upon these stories with disdain, thinking that a materialistic view is bound to lead to unhappiness. It is only the need to compensate for lack that leads men and women to think that the wealthy people are unhappy and lacking in spiritual qualities. An examination of the lives of the creative and successful will destroy this illusion once and for all.

Things Alone Are Not Security

Anyone who will think about it will come to the conclusion that real security is not in what is owned, but in the concept of life which is entertained by the individual. A man with the concept of wealth will manifest wealth. A man with a concept of health will do the right things, eat the right foods, get sufficient rest and relaxation in order to manifest health.

Some people come into large sums of money and they lose it because they do not know how to manage it. You must catch the awareness of being secure, regardless of present trends and circumstances, if you want to take command in this world. You must be able to initiate action, to make things happen, to be the motivating cause. You are either the effect of some outside stimulation or you are motivating someone else. Which will it be?

Dr. Paul P. Parker, author of *How to Use Tact and Skill in Handling People*,* says in his book, "When we see people who are successful, let us not assume that they are just lucky or got all the breaks. They made their own opportunities by keeping the right state of mind, by exercising their creative imagination and doing something about it." Be a doer. Make things happen!

Some of the most secure people I know own very little in the worldly sense but they are able to operate in this society and get what they want when they want it, which after all, is about all anyone has in mind.

These people learn to rely upon the "Infinite Invisible" to supply their every need. They have such a vivid realization of the hereness and nowness of everything that they are able to summon money, people, opportunity and situations at will . . . sometimes through channels which

* Published by Frederick Fell, Inc.

are quite unexpected. They think this way: "Basically there is only one substance in this world. Everything is energy, formed according to basic and definite patterns. Therefore, I can form this energy to suit my need if I can catch a mental picture of what it is I really want to experience."

Many thousands of people have been working with the concept popularized by the many metaphysical groups over the past hundred years. One need not be too aware to realize the significance of the concept that there is no such thing as matter separate from the Source. Spirit and matter is the false idea. Spirit as the world, as everything we behold, is the right idea. This brings the vision of oneness . . . this makes it possible for us to grasp the meaning of this chapter. When we see there is but one substance, appearing in many forms, then we can alter the forms to suit our desire, providing our desires are prompted from inner guidance and aligned with the right things for all concerned. No more do we have to be enslaved by the idea that matter controls us . . . we control matter by understanding its nature . . . as Spiritual substance only. This will bear some contemplation but the realization of it will be very liberating.

This ocean of mind-substance is constantly changing about us. The inner acceptance of a dream as being fulfilled will automatically will the means for its fulfillment. Dwell on this. Understand it. Doors will open, people will appear, opportunity will present itself . . . in response to your unspoken need.

Money isn't always the answer. Money can help you once you get into motion, but it will not dream for you or imagine new and more wonderful experiences. You can often realize your goal without money of your own. For instance, you have a product that you would like to expose to a nation-wide television audience. Perhaps you haven't got the money for a spot announcement; and besides, just one spot announcement wouldn't be sufficient—you would need a series of them in order to get your image over to the buying public. However, you might invest a modest fee in a good public relations firm that would in turn get you on any number of interview-type programs, if your product lent itself to this kind of exposure. In this way you would get more time than you could buy, do a better selling job because of the added human touch. And . . . at the same time you have rendered a service to the program on which you appeared because they need talent to keep on appealing to their viewers.

You may desire to live in a spacious home, yet lack the funds to buy one or keep it up. If you visualize yourself in the home of your desire, you will either be offered one that suits you, at a price you can afford . . . or you will be given one . . . or you will be invited to stay in one . . . or you may experience an unforeseen business increase that will enable you to buy at the going price. Every desire fulfills itself. This is the law of life. Knowing this, we ought to think in larger terms.

Expansion

You can enlarge your living area. You can move into greater fields of expression. What is it that enables some ministers to expand their work while others remain in the background, small and unnoticed? It is the mental attitude. I have known of ministers who would start a building project with no funds in the bank and no wealthy people to support the work, and yet, without strain everything goes forward. I know of a metaphysical church that wanted to purchase land next to the church building to use for a parking lot. The land was priced at $100,000. The board didn't announce their plan to the congregation; instead they retired as a group and "knew the truth" about this space and saw themselves already in possession of it. This was on a weekend. The following Monday morning a check arrived in the mail from a person who knew nothing of the project and who seldom came to church. It was made out for $100,000.

I firmly believe that we have to be open to inner guidance and be in step with the times. An idea that goes over this year may fail to go over next year. Make as many good solid contacts as you can and leave room for the unexpected to happen. When you begin to move in the direction of your dream, as though it were already fulfilled, doors will open and the world will stand by for you to pass.

Opportunity is always presenting itself. When I first came to the East Coast to lecture some years ago, I was unknown. I had never been here before. I did know of one man who had considerable experience in lecturing in the East. I wrote him a letter, listing my qualifications and offering to speak for him. An arrangement was made and I traveled from Los Angeles to Miami for a six-week lecture engagement which went over very well. This man also recommended me to groups in other major cities along the Atlantic Coast. Well-wishers advised me not to speak in these cities in the summer, for it was then early July, and anyone who has been in Washington, D.C., in July knows that it gets mighty warm.

I was too inexperienced to listen, and besides, I was sure I was doing the right thing. I made plans to speak in Washington, D.C., Philadelphia, New York City, Columbus and Cleveland. Each city opened beautifully and the lecture halls were filled to capacity. Not only this, but I appeared on radio and television interview shows in almost every city I visited. All this time I was visualizing myself as a wonderful success. I could not fail. I knew it.

After speaking for a number of years in the key cities of the East and after having published four books that sold quite well, I decided to include Los Angeles in my lecture tour for the near future. I had not been back since I left and I knew that in order to do well in Los Angeles I would have to reach a lot of people with good work. After deciding to go ahead with plans, I wrote to some friends and told them of my ideas, just to get the thoughts into circulation. I even picked the week that I would speak, some ten months from this time. This is what happened after I made the decision to go.

Inside of thirty days I received a letter from Mr. Jack Griffith of G. & J. Publishing in Hollywood. Mr. Griffith and his wife handle the book table in the lobby of the large and beautiful Grauman's Chinese Theater on Hollywood Boulevard. Mr. Griffith asked me if they could feature my book, *Time, Space and Circumstance*,* on their book table for the month of October. This was arranged and everything went well. Shortly after, in correspondence with Dr. Harry Douglas Smith, director of the Science of Mind Church which meets in the theater and with whom Mr. Griffith is associated, I was asked if I wanted to speak for them that coming summer. I checked my dates and found that the Sundays I would be speaking fitted perfectly with my schedule that was already arranged. I agreed to speak for two Sundays while in Los Angeles and both times the large audience was most responsive. Besides this arrangement, I spoke for two weeks for Dr. Smith on radio, appeared on television with Pamela Mason, and lectured several nights in Hollywood to the general public. In

* Published by Frederick Fell, Inc.

addition, my books sold so well that we had to order more from the wholesale house, which had been well supplied before my trip West.

I was particularly pleased with the outcome of this trip because I was able to reach so many hundreds of new people and also to work with an established group. This aided my work, gave it local support, and at the same time assisted the group for whom I spoke. Everyone was happy. This was, for me, the perfect working out of the plan, without strain or effort.

Accept Yourself

Feel at home where you want to be. This will give you confidence and will generate an aura of power about your person that will envelop all who come near you. The more you live from the center of your being, the more you will saturate yourself with this new vibration. When I speak of vibration I do not refer to anything vague or strange. We all know that some people have an aura which we can sense. Steve Allison, who is known as "the man who owns midnight" because of his late night radio show on WWDC in the nation's capital, calls this aura "magic." I have been on Steve's show many times and have heard him discuss this subject. Some show business personalities can turn it on and also turn it off. This "magic" is the difference between a drab performance and a great, sparkling show.

Too many people shuffle through life's pathway with an "excuse me for living" attitude. They feel guilty just for taking up space in this world. I'm told that most people, even those in high places, have moments when they feel they don't belong. Have you ever walked into the lobby of a plush hotel and felt yourself fade away until you were nothing? The bigness sort of overpowers you and makes you feel uncomfortable. If this is the case with you, then go there often until you can feel normal and at home in that environment. You can operate in any atmosphere if you feel normal in it. Bigness and littleness are a state of mind. Success and failure are a state of mind. Happiness and misery are a state of mind. Everything is projecting from your mental attitude. Later on in this book we will discuss how you can realize this and then alter your experiences just by "changing your mind" about them. But we have much ground to cover before we get to that point.

If you need experience in living in the realm you have chosen for yourself, then get out and get into contact with the environment and let the environment rub off on your subconscious. I don't wish to implant the idea that success is a matter of having bigger and better homes, status symbols and other trappings, nor is it a matter of living beyond your means. But I do believe that to be a success in this world you have to be able to handle any phase of it . . . and see yourself in the proper relationship to the whole thing.

Take Advantage of Opportunity but Not of a Person

A number of years ago, Marcus Bach, professor of the School of Religion at Iowa State University, was given a Rockefeller grant to investigate the little-known religious groups in the United States. One of the groups he investigated was the then active Psychiana mail-order organization, headed by Frank Robinson. Dr. Bach talked with Mr. Robinson at length. The latter's mail-order organization had been serving hundreds of thousands of believers but had also been given a hard time by the popular press

because of its unorthodox presentation. In the course of
the conversation, Mr. Robinson said, "They say I'm an
opportunist. Well, I admit it. The only thing that marks
me as different from the others is that I'm honest about it."

I think if we were honest about it we would admit to
being willing to accept opportunity also. It's all right to
take advantage of opportunity but not to take advantage of
a person. Prepare yourself, then grasp opportunity when it
presents itself. It has been said that luck is merely opportunity meeting up with preparation. Do be honest . . .
know what you want, then take it.

So many people deny themselves the good things of
life because they feel guilty about self-expression. I've
talked with women who weren't getting satisfaction from
their marriage because they were holding onto the illusion
that it wasn't right to enjoy a normal relationship with
their husband. I've talked with couples who remain in a
state of high tension for years because they are afraid to
take a vacation and leave the children with someone. Many
executives hold themselves back because they are reluctant
to streamline their work load; instead, they waste time and
energy in outmoded office procedures.

Remember to let others have the same freedom as you
desire to have. Your happiness does not have to come at
anyone else's expense. Imagine yourself surrounded by
Universal Mind, so responsive that whatever you think is
true gradually becomes true as this Mind molds to the
mental pattern. If we cannot get over thinking that we are
poor, sick and confused, we will remain poor, sick and
confused. As soon as we can picture ourselves as rich,
healthy and sure, the sooner this will come about for us.

No matter what happens to you, keep on expecting
more and more. Even when you think you have arrived,
just when you think you have attained all—from this

point launch out to greater things. No matter how large the picture in your mind, make it larger. If you want any experience you must grow until you are able to contain it. It may take time but you can do it.

REMEMBER TO PRACTICE:

1. Learn to see your world as you desire it to be, here and now.
2. Make provision only for success . . . not for failure.
3. Control your attention and get more out of life.
4. Rely upon the Infinite Invisible.
5. Take advantage of opportunity but not of people.
6. Get rid of the illusions that keep you from enjoying life.
7. Keep on expanding.

4

THE ART OF
RELEASING TENSION

It is very important that you know how to keep your emotions circulating and free from congestion. There is nothing wrong with feeling emotions; the trouble comes when they are dammed up and they have to break out the wrong way.

Life forces move through our bodies all the time. When these life forces are directed intelligently and we are able to live in a relaxed manner, we experience great joy and a wonderful sense of fulfillment. When energies are blocked off from certain areas of the body or are concentrated in one spot, we are bound to be on edge, nervous and hard to get along with.

We all know that at times we can experience an emotional release after dramatizing anger or some similar outburst, but this is not the best way to release dammed-up pressure. Far better to learn to release it constructively

68

without hurting ourselves or others. And this is the theme of this chapter.

Relax by Exploding Negative Ideas

Our emotions are connected to ideas and attitudes. We can find a connection between our feeling and our worries, grievances, resentments and annoyances. When you find this connection, just shift your viewpoint and clear up the attitude and you will automatically experience a release on the emotional level. You can take control of your life if you really want to. This basic decision to do so will outweigh all other superficial ideas and feelings.

Inadequate Expression Can Cause Tension

When you cannot, for some reason, express yourself as you would really like, you experience a building up of resistance which eventually brings tension and emotional congestion. Let us consider some of the possibilities in this line of thought.

Perhaps you are not getting satisfaction from your job. You feel that you are up against insurmountable obstacles. You cannot see your way out. You lack vision. You lack motivation. You get no support from your friends or family. The future looks bleak . . . and it is, as long as you stay in this pattern. You must change the pattern by beginning to catch the vision of what you can be and of what you can do, then you will move from your present situation.

Basically the idea is to relax and become still and mentally clear. Then use the technique of creative imagination to explore the wonderful world of the future. This will get you out of the rut and will help you to relax and

experience a release of tension. If you are stuck in a job
situation where you are dying on the vine, where no one
seems to be interested in your ability, then change your
job. Find your place in life and be supremely happy.

Malfunctioning Body Can Cause Tension

If your body isn't operating as it should, then do what
you need to do to get it in good shape. Do not put it off.
Sometimes we are afraid to go to the doctor for an examination because we are afraid of what he will find. We
secretly harbor thoughts of a serious problem. Often an
early checkup will clear the mind and allow you to return
to the job with a clear outlook. If there is something wrong,
you might as well get it cured as early as possible.

Some time ago I found myself in a situation similar
to what is implied here. I had been spending literally
hours from early in the morning until late at night getting
out a lot of correspondence and articles that were promised.
I began to notice a pain in my chest that seemed to come
and go and at times was more intense when I took a deep
breath. I could also feel my heart skip around now and then
in its beating. Now I believe that the body can be adjusted
to a great extent just by our altering the mental attitude.
But I also believe that if we see no change in a given
period of time, we ought to take more practical steps to
clear up the situation. After a few weeks with this condition I went to a doctor for a checkup. I was perfectly
sound in every respect. The only thing I had to do was to
get a little more rest and relaxation and sit straighter at
my desk. My constant posture, humped over the typewriter,
was the cause of the chest pains.

I once talked with a lady in New York City who

wanted me to tell her how to regenerate her teeth so as to avoid going to the dentist. Her motive was not so she could gain control over the processes of the body but so she could be free of the necessity of having the dentist hurt her when he filled her teeth. She didn't have the nerve to do what eventually had to be done to insure her health and comfort.

I am often confronted by people who want to correct some malfunctioning body part or organ by visualization techniques or by scientific prayer. While I do believe that the body reacts to right thinking and proper visualizing, I still think that a person would be wise to set a time limit for the healing. For instance, if you decide to clear up a condition by working from the mental and feeling level—and you can, for many of our physical problems are rooted in emotional discord—you should set a date in the near future for the absolute final moment for the healing. If, after this time, you have not relieved the condition you should seek professional help. You may be led to a psychologist, to a person who will help you with your diet, or to a physiotherapist. At any rate, you should do the practical thing to put your body in good working condition. This is only a common-sense attitude.

Inadequate Income

If your income is not what you think it should be you will be tense and worried. The pressure mounts as you are unable to pay your bills and meet the requests of those who depend upon you for support. The only solution in this case is to insure a larger income, one that is steady and consistent with proper and ethical practices. Begin to "see" yourself moving into larger areas of responsibility. "See" yourself handling the substance of this world. The chapter on money (Chapter Eight) will help solve any problems in this area.

Frustration Due to Stopping the Success Pattern

When you are engaged in a creative enterprise and something gets in the way—another person, a situation, lack of money, lack of public acceptance—and you know you can create but you are stopped in your tracks, you become frustrated. The only cure for this type of frustration is to move through the obstacles and experience the fulfillment of the creative cycle. When you are stopped repeatedly you tend to shut down your awareness and give up. You say that life is no good, there is no point in even trying. This is your defense against seemingly impossible obstacles.

You may be a salesman and you find that just when you get ready to close the sale you are unable to find the right words or feel the proper confidence in yourself and thus you lose out. You may be attracted to the wrong people, people who do not want your product or service in the first place. Then you must take stock of yourself and learn to assume the confident attitude necessary to be a successful salesman. You should check your leads and spend more time with people who do want your product or service and have the money to pay for it. This will solve your problem. It is also good if you can work with a product or service that gives you the feeling of having contributed to life as a result of your working with it.

You may be a writer and find that even though you have that great book in your head, it doesn't seem to take shape on paper. You may find little things getting in your way so that you fail to finish your manuscript. Here is where you need to discipline yourself and budget your time in order to produce and have the fulfilling experience of a job well done. You also have to learn to market your material so that you get rejection slips only now and then and you get your work published most of the time. We can all stand a few rejections but we need a lot of acceptance and a lot of recognition to balance them.

You may be a housewife and find that, try as you will, you cannot get your husband or the other members of the family to keep the house in good order. You will need to learn how to get them to cooperate by wanting to cooperate. This will take tact and skill but it can and should be done.

Or, like many other housewives you may find that you are confronted with the task of entertaining yourself while your husband, being the busy and upward-climbing executive, is away from home or shut off in his office or study. This can be a trying time for young wives who carry the idea in their minds that married life ought to be one continuous experience of togetherness. It may be that the husband is spending more time than is necessary away from you, tied up with his work. It will not help to scold and pout. Instead, be more understanding, more attentive, more cooperative. Take an interest in his business. Don't ask him to account to you for every second of his thinking and planning time but do be aware of what he is doing. You share in his success, so help him to it.

Loneliness in Companionship

Life has very little meaning to us unless we can share it with others. There is no reason why we should not find and mingle with the right people. We needn't cling to them or let them cling to us, but we can find the proper relationship.

It seems surprising that, in a world full of people, so many of them are alone. Many lonely people are either compulsive about trying to be friendly or they are hard to get along with when they do strike up a new friendship. The best way to attract and keep friends is to be friendly and yet be independent. Friendly self-reliance is attractive. Enjoy being a friend but do not be a burden by showing that you need friends.

One of the big fears among older people is that they will spend their years alone. This need not be the case at all if our senior citizens will continue to be interested in the world and maintain an attractive and pleasant personality. The wrong way to go about it is to demand that younger members of the family pay respect to the older members when the older members do nothing to warrant it. Understanding there should be, but how much better it is when there is a good working relationship among all members of the family and community as a result of everyone's being in harmony.

A hint for the lonely people of the world: try to see that Life is being the true friend *through* the people you meet. This way you will lose the urge to cling to individuals and, instead, meet many new and wonderful people at every turn of the way.

Young women who seek the proper companionship should frequent places where they are likely to meet the right men. They should be sure they are well groomed and attractive, poised and attentive, interested and interesting. If you are a lonely woman and you are seeking companionship, are you doing the right things . . . are you spending time with the right people? I know of young women who want to get married. Yet they persist in keeping company with men who are either already married or whose religion will not allow them to marry women of a different faith. This attitude in a woman shows that subconsciously she may want a man but she does not want to be married.

There is still much ignorance and superstition about the male-female relationship—too many instances of otherwise mature men and women acting coy and childish in their relationship with each other. Women are attracted to men just as much as men are to women and I see no reason for the woman to sit around the apartment waiting for the man to call her just because she thinks it is his place to do so. Is there any reason why she shouldn't call him? Is there any reason why she shouldn't take the initiative at times? In this age of feminism many men are put on the defensive and a positive motion on the part of the woman would put them at ease. A woman cannot be a man but she can be a whole woman, which is much better. I think that women who are on a crusade for their rights are very insecure. I read recently that "The feminist who campaigns for 'involvement' with mankind will most always admit that involvement with one man is her ultimate goal."

I have also noticed that many women who seek God and Truth with such intensity so as to be overemphasizing it, would be much happier if they would concentrate on a normal relationship with a suitable man.

The worst thing to do if you are seeking companionship is to join clubs and groups which are set up to bring lonely people together. All you will meet at these places are other people who are lonely. It is a pretty desperate situation. To get out of the pit of loneliness you must begin to mingle with people who are not lonely, who are contented and who have found their place in life . . . then you will be carried along in this mental atmosphere.

The Importance of Sexual Maturity

It is surprising how few people are really mature in their outlook and behavior where sex is concerned. The treatment of this subject in our novels, movies and newspapers is not always as wholesome as it should be. But I am glad to see evidence, in spite of the front that we put up about how embarrassed we are even to think of sex— that, beneath the surface, people are learning to work out their problems and are learning to deal with their urges in a natural way.

A great many men and women have a double standard. They speak one way so as to be accepted by their friends as being proper, and then they go right on and discreetly do what they want to do. Where people who live this way are psychologically sound we see no evidence that it has any ruinous effects on their lives. It is only when guilt and a puritanical sense of evil accompanies normal sexual relationships that we find trouble manifesting itself. Whatever two mature people decide to do in their relationship with each other is normal, as long as they enter into the relationship with full understanding and cooperation and there is no one on the sidelines who will be hurt because of their doing so.

Every now and then we find crusaders trying to get a law passed to ban books and magazines from the public newsstands. I often wonder what kind of relationship these zealous people have at home. If their actions are prompted by evidence that such true-to-life publications are harmful to young minds then perhaps they have a case. But if they are driven by a terrible compulsion to remove books and articles of a sex-orientated nature from the gaze of others it must represent some dark and perverted areas in their own mental processes.

It is normal to desire a warm human relationship and it is normal to enjoy such a relationship. In the perfect relationship it is not a matter of give and take—it is a matter of sharing, of two people becoming one. This is ideal and can be realized more often than not if men and women will be free and spontaneous with each other. A normal sex life can be a great tension reliever because it makes a person feel one with his environment, and the more we can be in tune with our environment the healthier we will be. Just having a sexual experience is not enough, because mere release of built-up tension which springs from desire will not give the deep feeling of at-one-ness. The ideal situation exists when two people can find the perfect relationship and complete fulfillment in it. Then they have peace. They balance each other perfectly.

When our emotional life is regulated we can work better. We can take our attention from the need for emotional satisfaction and turn it to constructive enterprises. A person who is well adjusted sexually will be more likely to be well adjusted in work and other activities. A person who is not well adjusted sexually will find more often than not that he has sex on his mind a lot of the time and this detracts from his creative work.

Redirection of the Sex Urge

We have already concluded that it is a far healthier situation for a person to have a normal emotional relationship with a member of the opposite sex. If this, for some reason, is not possible, then the alternative must be a redirection of the sex urge. It is futile for anyone to try to remove sex desire . . . in fact, it is extremely unwise to do so, because this powerful drive can be directed into new channels. If it is suppressed it will merely force its way out in some other area, as thoughts and feelings of desire, erotic dreams and flights of fancy, even as puritanical behavior. Many people who suppress this urge become cold and hard to live with. They argue and scold and pick fights with friends, neighbors and members of their own family. They often accept a doctrine which holds celibacy to be a virtue in order to support their loveless existence.

On the other hand, many people have learned to successfully transmute this creative urge and produce outstandingly well in their work, in the creative arts, in bringing harmony and beauty to their environment. Most of our really successful men and women have had great magnetism, which is the result of their highly sex-charged natures. This magnetism is revealed in their vibrant handshake, the tone of their voice, their good posture and body movements, their quality of thoughts and their manner of caring after their personal appearance.

Look at any of our leaders and see if they do not have sex appeal, that magnetism that we are talking about. When you try to erase this magnetism and deny the fact that you are a full-blooded man or woman you live only half a life. Learn to identify with the object of your desire in a creative sense and transmute the urge for sexual expression into noble creations in this world. Learn to redirect this drive and you will succeed beyond your fondest dreams.

Balanced Interchange the Secret

There are some men, as well as women, who cannot seem to get enough sex experience. They are either psychologically unbalanced or they have not learned to give themselves fully to the other partner and share in the electric interchange which alone can bring emotional balance in the sexual relationship. When this problem is overcome, when men and women learn to share completely, there is a release of tension as the energies of the body are balanced out and real fulfillment is experienced. The idea that normal sexual experience is evil, harmful or wasteful is completely unfounded. Such ideas are spread and sustained by people who have not experienced fulfillment in this area.

Suggestions for Complete Relaxation

Perhaps you have found that the harder you try to relax, the more difficult it is to do so. You may have been keyed up and the mental decision to relax was not sufficient to induce that soothing release you looked for. As long as the mind is active, as long as the energies are tied up in the deeper recesses of the body, there can be no relaxation. I will suggest a number of ways for you to relax and you can select the methods that seem best for you.

Often, all we have to do to relax is to break from our present pattern for a while to be free of the pressures and strains incidental to them. A change of pace is relaxing. It gives us a chance to re-create our energies and vital forces.

1. Learn to be aware of the body. Accept it. It is your vehicle through which you express yourself. Do not reject your body and think of it as a necessary evil. Do not be ashamed of it. Learn to gently tense and feel every area of your body. Massage your skin. Stretch and twist and turn, all the while feeling the body awaken and come alive. Too many people lose communication with their body . . . they are ashamed of it and drag it around through life. In this enlightened age there is no need for this negative mental attitude. Rejection of the body is the cause of many accidents. It is the cause of many psychosomatic ills. It is the

reason why people do not take care of the body and why they deny it proper nutrition and exercise and rest. I am not advocating that you develop a body complex, but I do suggest a healthy attitude in regard to it.

2. Now, realize that your body is sustained by life force. This life force is in the air you breathe and in the food you eat; it is all around you. You can even take it in by an act of will. Notice how much more energetic you are when you like your work, when you are thrilled with the anticipation of some creative enterprise. When you maintain a balance in your activities and keep the right mental attitude, you can experience a flow of vital life force and never tire or wear out the body. Whatever you do, do willingly.

3. Take a brisk walk every day. This will improve the circulation of the blood and keep you alert. When you walk, for health's sake walk with vigor and purpose. Be precise. Be confident. Be alive. Maintain a fully erect posture. Breathe in fully and exhale completely. Be in tune with life.

4. Realize that there is an innate intelligence which knows how to adjust the body. I am not speaking of anything mysterious at all. I am speaking of the Intelligence that created the body in the first place. This body was created according to a specific pattern and if we can remove the tensions and inner conflicts there is no reason why the body cannot be maintained according to the perfect pattern.

The secret of healing is to prepare the way so that the healing forces can work without interruption. Medical science today recognizes that a great many of our ailments have their origin in a distorted emotional life and in deep-seated tensions. Tensions distort our feeling patterns and this breeds conflict. The life forces cannot flow through these tension barriers and do their work. The greatest way to come alive is to learn to relax and let the healing life currents move through the body as they should.

The Secret of Deep Relaxation

At least once a day, seek out a quiet place. Release any tight or restricting garments. Remove the shoes. Wear as little as possible. Then, lie down on the floor and relax as best you can. Feel the weight of the body . . . sink into the floor . . . relax . . . relax . . . relax. Now comes the interesting part of the process. While you are practicing for the next twenty-five to thirty minutes, just relax and see if you can release any conscious mind effort to will this relaxation . . . do not do anything to make yourself relax and do not do anything to prevent any free body movements, such as stretching, twisting, turning. Just let the body do what it wants to do. This may sound strange in the beginning but you just try it and see what happens. Let the body take over. Remember, we mentioned earlier that the body had an inner intelligence? Let it run the session.

If the body wants to stretch and yawn, let it. If the body wants to roll about and change position, let it do so. If it wants to sleep, this is all right . . . but be sure not to make any conscious effort to do these things. Relax and feel the life forces deep within as they awaken and begin to surge through the body. Feel them circulate and warm your being. There may be mild trembling as these energies come alive, there may be vocal expression such as sighing, or there may be deep and abiding peace. The end result after several days of faithful practice will be a peace and power that cannot be denied—a sense of physical, mental and spiritual well-being that will be uplifting and joyous. This practice does not take the place of entering the creative silence, which we will discuss in the next chapter, but it does help you along in the right direction . . . because the more you can relax, the more effective you will be in your efforts to enter the creative silence.

The above-described method of relaxing has been termed the unconscious method of relaxation. Try it. You will find that it is a great help to living a more creative life.

Further Aids to Relaxation and the Release of Tension

Thousands of men and women are today learning the value of the ancient science of yoga. The true purpose of yoga is to teach one to still the mind and enter the creative silence. As a step in this direction, a practitioner of yoga often engages in the yoga postures, which are a series of stretching and twisting movements that aid in the flushing of toxins from the system, relaxes the muscles on every level of the body and restores peace of mind. Many popular books are available at the library or through your book dealer which will describe the postures in detail.

The main thing to remember as you practice them is to catch the mental picture of yourself doing the postures before you perform them, and in this way there will be no difficulty. They are especially helpful as they enable one to get at the deeper muscles that are ordinarily not worked upon in the usual freehand exercises.

Mental Relaxation

Probably the most important thing to remember is that mental relaxation precedes physical relaxation. Learn to identify with the rules of positive living and you will then be at peace, and this peace will reflect in your physical body. Cast out fear and anxiety. Accept faith and confidence into your life. It can work a miracle.

REMEMBER TO PRACTICE:

1. Explode negative ideas and attitudes.
2. Get rid of emotional congestion.
3. Grow up emotionally in relationship to sex.
4. Learn to transmute the creative urge.
5. Practice deep relaxation every day.
6. Relaxation starts in the mind; keep it clear.

5

ERASING THE PAINFUL PAST

In the last chapter we were discussing the importance of clearing up emotional congestion. One of the causes of emotional congestion is found in our reaction to what we believe to be an injustice. When someone with more influence takes advantage of us or abuses us in some way, we often experience a hurt which is often hard to get rid of. We cannot fight back but we can bear a grudge. We can feel beaten and bitter.

While we may harbor these feelings we can also realize that they can do us no good if we retain them. We must get rid of them if we are to function freely. If we are confident enough we can rise above the seeming injustice and go right ahead with our plans. If we feel persecuted, we must get rid of this feeling. Common sense often isn't sufficient to enable us to shake the feeling. We must do

84

something more. And this something more is to revise the painful memory.

Memories are recorded as pictures, loaded with energy, on the subconscious level. Especially is this true of memories of emotional experiences. Now, there is no real need to erase the memory of any experience, but we can erase the pain which is tied in with it, thus we can look objectively at past experiences and relate them to present and future plans. The easiest method to shake the pain is to just relax and see through it and let it go.

If you find this impossible, then try the technique of revision.

Revision

When you revise something you change it or modify it. This is what you are to do with your painful memories. Put them in their place. There is no reason to hang on to the pain of a past experience and have it get in the way of your living in the present. First . . . be willing to face the fact that you want to get rid of the pain. Be sure there isn't any deep-seated need to play a martyr role, a need to experience pain to justify your existence. Then retire to a quiet place. Relax just as you would were you to begin the practice of the technique of creative imagination. Drift back in your mind's eye to the moment when you experienced the psychic shock, the rejection, the unjust act. Feel the pain that went with it . . . don't try to avoid it. You must face it if you are to get rid of it.

You can do one of two things at this point. You can replay the scene in your mind's eye, with full feeling, not as it did happen but as you wished it had happened. You will not change the past but you will erase the pain recording which is connected to the memory. When you relive it this way a few times with feeling, you can then come out of your reverie state and look at the past situation without the emotional reaction that once accompanied it. This gives you release. It enables you to release any feelings of animosity concerning another and it enables you to look ahead with all of your energies at your disposal. When you have these pain patterns etched on the subconscious level, you are literally loaded down with the weight of the past, and this overload keeps you from expressing as freely as you should. When you get this release you will find tremendous reserves of energy being released for your direction and use.

Another technique that you might find easier to use is this: when you get to the point in the silence where you are faced with the full impact of the pain and memory . . . then just look at it and take long . . . deep . . . breaths of air. Breathe deeply . . . several times . . . while looking at the memory and feeling the pain. This will blow the emotional charge out of the memory so that you can look at the incident, chalk it up to experience and let it go.

Why is this so?

The body likes to perform the functions that are closely connected with survival. Hence we experience pleasure when we eat, when we make love, when we are secure in our environment, when we breathe. Breathing is very important for the body, hence it has prime survival value for the body. When you put the body to the test and cause it to choose between performing an important function and experiencing pain, it will choose the former every time. So, just breathe deeply and regularly for several minutes and you will find the emotional pain begin to discharge.

I once met a lady who had been left out of her stepfather's will. She was hurt because she took this as an indication of his lack of love for her. For years she carried this pain of rejection in her heart. It dominated her conversation, it stood between her and her good times. She told me that a friend had advised that she just accept it as her cross to bear. I told her to practice this breathing exercise when she felt overcome with the pain . . . and it wasn't long before she began to come out of that pattern and take an interest in life.

I know of many businessmen who fail. They think they have been rejected by the business community or that they have failed to go along with the rules of the community and were closed down. They lost a lot of money and they are hurt and bitter. This cannot help them regain their money or their position. They need to identify with successful people. They need to move into a position of influence, they need to envision great things for the future and then move into their dreams. They cannot take the pain of rejection and failure with them or it will modify their plans and inhibit them. The best thing for them to do is to erase the pain as we have outlined here and then recall past successes and identify with thoughts and ideas and feelings which will spell success for them.

Erase the Past by Living in the Present

When you allow yourself to live in the memory of the past you are "stringing yourself out through time" and this is a great waste. Learn to look around you and take an interest in life. Begin to get involved in some worthwhile activity. Synchronize your feelings, thoughts and actions in line with your ideals. When you do this you are moving in the right direction with your whole being. You are living in the moment, looking forward to the wonderful future, and this is a healthy condition.

Take stock of yourself in the present. What are your talents? What can you do? What would you like to do? Then prepare for it. Read about others who are doing it. Begin to catch the feelings that will be yours when you begin to move into the larger picture. The only way out is into a new and larger realization of life. Make your move.

You may need to change your living habits. Change your reading material. Change your manner of dressing. Change your routine. Maybe you will begin to spend your leisure time to better advantage. You may even change your name. This may sound a bit shocking to some people, but bear in mind that it has been done to the apparent advantage of the person. It isn't that a mere change of name will make the difference, but you may move into a new level of awareness as you assume the new role. You are always playing a role anyway until you arrive at that point of supreme self-discovery, so why not play a role that suits you? Many businessmen use just the first initial and the middle and last name. Or, they use two initials and the last name. Authors and other people in the public eye often experiment until they find the right way to use their name so that it conveys the proper image.

Everything we do is revealed in our manner of walking, talking and speaking. Even our handwriting reveals a lot. You may want to compare your handwriting now with the way you used to write. When you are optimistic you tend to write in a bold hand and when you are negative you tend to waver and have a downward slant to your characters. The story is told that Napoleon, early in his career, signed his name Napoleon Bonaparte. When he began to be more influential he signed his name as Napoleon. When he reached the peak of his power he signed simply, Nap. As his influence declined he used his whole first name again.

Notice successful and outgoing people when they autograph books or sign letters. They do so with a flourish. This is an outward sign of their inner nature. Move out. Begin to extend yourself and get in tune with life. Any of the little things you can successfully use will be helpful.

Destroy Existing Ideas That Stand in the Way

By using the simple technique as set forth in this book you will be able to understand the creative laws of life. Knowing about them is not the same as applying them.

REMEMBER TO PRACTICE:

1. Revise the past through visualization.
2. Release the emotional pain through breathing.
3. Cancel the past by living in the present.
4. Synchronize your feelings, thoughts and actions in the right way.

6

ENTERING THE CREATIVE SILENCE

You cannot be fully creative unless you learn to enter the realm of creativity and this is best done in the silence. Without knowing how to enter the creative silence you can only go so far on the ladder of self-unfoldment, but with it—you will find undreamed of possibilities opening to you.

I am stressing the idea of creative silence because too often we tend to think of going into the silence as a negative experience. It is my intention to explain this process of entering the creative silence so well as to enable you to enter into it and see such results flow forth as a consequence that you will never give it up.

Why Should We Desire to Enter the
Creative Silence?

When we learn to go into the creative silence we can detach ourselves from this world at will. Too many people are breaking down today because they are carrying the accumulated load of tension and psychic pain. When they learn to drop this load and come into a new awareness of life, they can relate this new understanding to everyday situations. They can then tap the realm of new and revolutionary ideas. Unleash heretofore locked up masses of energy and direct it into proper and productive channels. People who gain release from narrow viewpoints can also receive guidance, learn to relax and make peace with the environment.

How to Enter the Silence

If you have never practiced in the silence this instruction may sound a bit strange in the beginning. It really isn't too difficult and practice will show you that it is quite helpful.

Choose a place where you can be alone for at least thirty minutes a day . . . but be able to extend this time to an hour. You may use your study, your office, your bedroom. Wherever you decide to practice be sure it is quiet and well ventilated.

Then, walk back and forth a few minutes and stretch and relax. Loosen your belt, necktie or other tight garments. You may also want to remove your shoes. Then, sit upright in a comfortable chair so that you feel you can remain in it for the next thirty minutes or so. Have your back away from the chair and your feet either flat on the floor or arranged comfortably.

Be sure you are balanced and relaxed. Your head should be upright and in line with your spine. Hands can be folded on the lap or resting on the thighs. Breathe deeply for a minute or two . . . then inhale . . . hold it . . . exhale . . . relax. This will help you to break from any tension and will also help to break the train of thoughts. Just relax and be aware . . . direct your attention to the point or area just behind the forehead, inside. Be aware that you are sitting in a relaxed attitude. Mentally release any feelings of guilt, regret, failure, dislike, fear or anxiety. Release yourself from any feelings of tensions relating to projects or goals.

Be content to rest in the silence. Your experience in the silence will better help you to confront life's problems, so practice well. Watch the activity of the mind and body in a detached manner. When you feel the mind beginning to wander off, the body beginning to tense up, take a long deep breath of air and let it go with a gentle sigh and relax . . . resume your concentration for as long as you are comfortable.

How to Control the Mind

Be content to let the thoughts run through the mind. Let them go for a while and watch them. Make no attempt to control them at this time. Be content to let the body breathe and function as it will. Just observe the process, always keeping the attention up in the area of the forehead. This in itself is good practice and will take you deeper into the silence. This is not an auto-conditioning process and it is not self-hypnosis . . . and you are not to go to sleep. You are to be aware at all times.

What is taking place? First, you are sitting in the silence. You are relaxed. And, being in the silence in this manner, with the attention lifted to the point in the mid-forehead, you begin to be aware of energies in the body as they are released, flowing back to the spine and into the brain. As this happens you find that you are disconnected from the world and your mind is free to be engaged in creative work. This reversal of the flow of life force takes place gradually in the beginning, but after a while, with practice, it is just like turning a switch.

As the muscles relax and the life forces flow back to the spine and brain, the heart and lungs have fewer demands made upon them and they also slow down. This releases more life force which is not needed and it too is free to flow to the brain. Thus, free of the restricting demands of the body, you are able to explore the worlds within.

A Psycho-Physical Technique

Why do we suggest concentration at the point between the eyebrows or behind the forehead? Because, when we concentrate at this point we tend to direct the flow of energies into this area. The energies in the body flow wherever the attention is directed. When we are aware of the body, as we usually are, we are also aware of the immediate environment and the problems connected with the body and environment. When you focus your attention as I suggest here, it is much easier to remain in a clear state of mind, free from distraction.

Notice the relationship between the level of the eyes and the outlook on life. When you are depressed and moody, your eyes are usually downcast . . . as you are attuned to the subconscious level of your mind, the storehouse of memories and habit patterns. When you look straight ahead you tend to identify with the moment and think clearly from present time observations. When the eyes are lifted a bit you tend to push into areas of inspiration. Try it. When you are discouraged or feel blue, lift your eyes, lift your focus of attention and see if your spirits do not rise. You will find that you do feel a lift in consciousness and that you do get some control over your mental attitude.

This is not merely due to my suggestion. Try it on a friend who is feeling sorry for himself . . . who is despondent. Ask him to lift his eyes for a few moments and you will see him brighten and take on a new light and a new interest.

How Breath, Mental Activity and Life Forces Are Interconnected

One of the simple things to remember is this: the act of breathing, the mental activity and the flowing of energy in the body go together. If you can control the mind, the breath or the flow of energy, in any combination, you have the secret of self-mastery in your hands.

The restless mental activity is the reason for the restless breathing and the restless feelings in the body. The next time you are restless in body or mind, try this: stand upright, take a full deep breath, hold it, tense the body for a moment, then relax and throw the breath out. When you release the breath let it go with a sigh, and relax. Do it again, inhale . . . tense gently, throw the attention to the point between the eyebrows, relax and exhale. See how relaxed you are . . . and in control of your mental activities? You can be the master of your body and mind if you decide to be the master.

Do not allow yourself to be distracted against your will. Always be in full control of yourself in every situation. If you allow yourself to be carried away by your feelings you will lose control of your thoughts and become confused. Always be in full control of your feelings. This does not mean that you cannot have emotion, but be the master and not the slave of your emotional life.

Wherever you direct your attention, you tend to create your world. The secret of success in any line of endeavor is to direct your attention into the proper channels. A man with ability to concentrate can accomplish in days what the average man takes weeks to do. The secret of getting things done in this life is to condense experience through concentration and directed attention . . . thus you telescope time.

How Will This Help Me?

This is a direct question that needs to be answered. When you learn to sit quietly in the silence, releasing all emotional conflict, all tension and anxiety, even all desire, you experience peace. You are fully at rest. You get released from the pressures of the day and have the opportunity to be objective. Also, you clear the tensions and make it possible for yourself to receive guidance as to how best to handle life situations. When you allow pressure to mount up, the time must come when something has to give. Far better to learn the art of consciously resting in tune with the Universal Life.

This is a realization that many men come to . . . that they are living in a vibrant, intelligent universe. A universe that can be a wonderful place in which to live. A universe that is not malevolent but which is willing to cooperate with us.

We also become more intuitive. Intuition is the power of knowing directly, without recourse to inference or reasoning. We should sit in the silence and know that the Spirit of Life is directing us at all times. We should try to feel that our thought is permeated by the Infinite Intelligence. We should expect to be directed but not become discouraged if the direction does not come right away. We must learn to have absolute reliance upon this inner movement in consciousness until we learn to recognize truth that is revealed.

Contemplate the Desirable

Earlier we mentioned that man becomes what he contemplates. Many writers have said the same thing with different words, but it is still the same truth. In the silence you may contemplate any one or a number of desirable attributes until they become a part of your nature. You may contemplate serenity, peace of mind, kinship with all life, your right place in life. Wherever your attention is directed, there you will identify. You become that which you contemplate. Therefore, contemplate the desirable qualities and partake of them. You can be the person you want to be.

When you go into the creative silence in the early part of the day you get yourself in tune with the world and you step out with a feeling of optimism and faith. When you go into the creative silence* at night, just before going to sleep, you cancel out the tensions and conflicts that might have come up during the day and you are able to go to sleep with a clear mind and enjoy a night of refreshing rest.

Find Yourself in the Silence

A very helpful thing to do is to find your center of balance while in the silence. This can best be done as you rest and just look within . . . observing the way you think, the way you feel, the way you seem to react to life situations. Do not find fault, just observe yourself from the inside. It is quite a revealing experience and will enable you to handle yourself better in your environment.

* For further information on entering the creative silence, read the chapter "How to Meditate" in the author's book, *Time, Space and Circumstance*, published by Frederick Fell, Inc.

So enter the silence . . . relax . . . be aware . . . be your true self . . . and enjoy it.

REMEMBER TO PRACTICE:

1. Have a quiet place for your practice.
2. Understand the relationship between mental activity and breath.
3. Try the psycho-physical technique for controlling your mental attitude.
4. Contemplate the desirable qualities and make them your own.
5. Experience self-discovery . . . and rejoice!

7

HOW TO RECEIVE GUIDANCE

One of the most satisfying things in the world is to know that you are in your right place in life. And the best way to know this is to seek guidance by learning to listen to the inner promptings of intuition. When you find your place in life you suddenly realize that all resistance is melting and the effort is going out of living. Until you find your right place you are bound to hit snags and obstacles as a result of your inner darkness.

To receive guidance we do not have to be inclined toward the mystical things of life, though a true mystic is a person who sees clearly. We have but to learn to be open by being willing to know the truth about our right place in life. Too often we tend to live according to someone else's idea of what is good for us. We may accept the well-meaning advice of a parent or a friend, or we may uncon-

sciously identify with a childhood ideal . . . only to find
that later on we are not living our life but someone else's.

Or we may have a tendency to dwell in the past and
ignore the present. Then again we may worry about the
future, the future that will never be. Either way we deny
ourselves the best that life has to offer.

Living in the Wonderful Now

Now is the only real time there is. You may remember yesterday or a whole string of yesterdays and you may
contemplate the tomorrows, but you can only be aware of
now. Why not enjoy it? The more aware you are, the more
you will understand the nature of the mind and the more
successful you will be. Look around you . . . observe people, nature, things . . . I mean really observe. Pretty wonderful, isn't it?

How to Receive Guidance in the Silence

Because of the many distractions which are pressing
in upon us during our everyday living, we tend to ignore
the whispering of the inner voice of guidance. I firmly believe that since we are part of the larger picture, we have
a place in it and we can find it if we will open ourselves to
guidance. When we do this we become aware of the whole
situation, including those areas which are usually hidden
from our conscious view.

Many outstanding people have learned to receive
guidance from within. Charles Fillmore, one of the found-
ers of the large and prospering Unity movement, sought
guidance early in his career. Many times he did not know
which way to turn for help . . . for advice on how to direct
his growing organization. So, at night, before retiring he

would bring before his mind's eye all the known factors
of a problem and then turn it over to a greater Intelligence.
During the hours of sleep he would either have a dream,
which he would remember upon awakening and which
would contain the answer to his question or the solution to
his problem; or at times he would merely awaken with the
answer that he needed. If he did this in the middle of the
night he would turn on the bedside lamp and write his idea
down on a pad of paper which he kept for that purpose.
Otherwise it might slip from his mind.

When we learn to turn within for guidance we are not
shirking our responsibility at all. Sometimes you find that
you cannot think a problem through because you have a
mental or emotional block. Inner tension prevents our having the answer slip into the forefront of the mind. The will
to know, plus relaxation, triggers off the mental mechanism
and we have access to areas of mind which are usually
screened off.

Techniques

1. Get guidance while you sleep. When you retire, do
so with all the known factors of a problem assembled before your mind's eye and set your mental attitude so that
you expect to get the answer. Then, go to sleep. As you
sink into the sleep state you pass through various levels of
awareness and at one point you will make contact with the
storehouse of all knowledge, the mighty superconscious
mind . . . and at this point the right answer will be presented to the conscious mind so that when you awaken it
will be right there for you to see. The key to this technique
is expectancy.

2. Sometimes you get guidance while you are in the
dream state. When you pass through the area of mind men-

tioned above, the truth of what you seek will translate itself into the form of a dream, either symbolic or an actual dramatization which you will recall when you awaken. Scientists and writers have had complex formulas and plots presented to them in this way. Men and women have had glimpses of loved ones at a distance and . . . if we are to believe the records, military leaders have gotten precise instructions as to how to plan important battles . . . all while in the dream state.

The reason we get the guidance while in the dream state and not in the conscious state is that when we are awake and conscious we tend to reject the obvious. Or, the mental activity cancels out the intuition.

3. Another method of getting guidance is to expect to get the answers to all of life's problems from life itself. I favor this method. Recognize that life is one. Only to the eye of the uninitiated does it appear to be divided. We live in an ocean of mind and we draw whatever we need, when we need it, providing we have eyes to see and ears to hear. You may get the answer to a question from a chance remark of a friend or from a total stranger. You may open a book seemingly by chance and there it is, or you may hear the words to a song, get an intuitive flash out of the blue—either way it comes, it comes at the right time. However you accept your guidance, you can have it. Opportunity is all around us, it is a matter of our opening our eyes so we can see it. The mental attitude makes all the difference in the world. When every door seems to be closed, look again . . . train yourself to see the open door. You will find, as have others, that often it is not so much a matter of making anything happen or of going anywhere or of doing anything . . . as it is seeing the obvious.

4. Make it a practice to carry some index cards or a small notebook. When you have an idle moment and an

idea flashes into your mind, jot it down before it fades away. After you receive such a flash you may want to let it ripen a bit before acting upon it . . . just to see if it still looks good after you have thought it over. Do not mistake every hunch for a direct revelation from the Infinite, because you can get impressions from the subconscious as well as the superconscious levels. With practice you will be able to tell the difference between a subconscious urge and an intuitive or superconscious flash. Usually the flash fairly sizzles and you tingle all over. Practice will make perfect. You may want to select a time of day to sit down and open yourself for guidance. Often the guidance you get is a flow of just plain common sense that you didn't know you had until you gave yourself a chance.

5. When you sit down on purpose to receive guidance, sit with a pencil ready and say to yourself, "Where do I go from here?" Or, "This is the problem as it appears to be (state it), now what is the solution?" If you relax, from the recesses of your mind will come the answer. Not just any answer but the one that fits your particular situation. Are you stymied? Sit for guidance and see what happens. When you get it, act upon it. Do what you feel led to do. Put it to the test, for this will confirm it.

6. It is hard for some people to get a flow of ideas started if they have had no experience along this line. We are so used to being helpless and undecided that it is difficult to assume the right mental attitude that will trigger off the flow of ideas. If this is true for you, then identify with a point of contact. Do you know of someone who might know what it is you want to know? Then relax and bring them before your mind's eye and ask them for advice. Oh, you needn't worry about getting an answer or about contacting them telepathically; just get the impression of what their viewpoint might be concerning the subject. After all,

this is what you want. When you can see life through their eyes you can know what they know.

We all do this unconsciously anyway. We have, in the back of our mind, the image of someone we admire, someone who has been an inspiration to us. We draw power from this image, we identify with it and it gives us purpose and direction in life. Napoleon Hill, in his masterful book *Think and Grow Rich*, tells of how, for years, he met with his "Invisible Counselors" and over a period of time he was able to take on some of their characteristics. In his mind he contacted Emerson, Paine, Edison, Darwin, Lincoln, Burbank, Napoleon, Ford and Carnegie. Each one of these nine men acted as a point of contact for Mr. Hill and enabled him to see life from a new viewpoint. It made him a fuller, richer person. Each night before he went to sleep he would bring this band of men before his inner vision, in his imagination. He would seat them around a conference table and he served as chairman. He would put questions to them and get their views, through his own notions of what they might say . . . and he was thus guided through several trying periods of his life.

We have all used this technique to some extent, perhaps without conscious intent. I can recall my early years on the lecture platform when I would be asked questions for which I was not prepared. I would relax and recall how I felt when I saw someone speaking on this particular subject. Then, by a process of identification with this person I seem to tap into the stream of thoughts to which he had access and in almost all cases come up with the right answer.

It is no longer strange for executives to admit that they sit for ideas. In fact, the method is being introduced to an ever increasing number of them through such books as this one, through recordings and through seminars which are set up for the purpose.

7. While it is good that we know the various methods of getting guidance, we should bear in mind that the best way to know anything is simply to know it. We can learn to operate so that we have the answers all of the time, right in the forefront of the mind. The best way to know anything is to want to know ... then believe you have the capacity to know.

Many insights come without conscious planning on our part. They well up from the depths of the mind. Dr. Walter B. Cannon of Harvard investigated the creative habits of 232 high-ranking chemists and found that more than a third of them gave credit to these inner illuminations or flashes of insight.

You have to prepare yourself for success. You have to prepare yourself mentally for successful thinking. You have to look forward to operating intuitively. This will pre-condition you to the idea.

So, start now. Try the methods that seem best to you and see what happens.

REMEMBER TO PRACTICE:

1. Live in the ever-present now ... with an eye to the future.
2. Try the techniques.
3. Raise your level of expectancy.
4. Use some ideal as a "point of contact."
5. Assume that you can know.

8

MONEY—WHAT IT IS AND HOW TO HAVE PLENTY OF IT

Maybe this chapter heading startled you. If it repelled you then you probably need to know what I'm going to say. You may have subconscious blocks which are keeping you from the wonderful experiences you claim to want. In line with our philosophy that man can have any experience that he will contemplate and accept, we find that the subject of money is quite compatible. To be able to handle money you have to be able to accept the responsibility of handling it. You have to acquire a "money-consciousness."

Let's do some straight thinking about this concept of money. We all handle money in our everyday experience and we ought to understand what money is. Money is a medium of exchange. When you render a service to someone you receive payment in the form of money. Money is a convenient form in which to receive and store your service

units. You can accumulate your service units and exchange
them for things you want. It gives you great flexibility.

Service in Quality and Quantity

On one level of operation you can make your life
prosperous and satisfying by finding how to serve your fellow man in quantity and quality, for which he will compensate you with his service units or dollars. The greater your
service in quantity and quality . . . the greater should be
your return.

With our expanding population there is an ever-in-
creasing market for true service. Don't waste your time
figuring out how to exploit your fellow man . . . figure how
you can service his needs and you will have secured your
fortune. Serve in small measure and you receive in small
measure . . . serve in large measure and you will receive
in large measure. What are you contributing to life? How
large is your concept of life?

Getting Behind the Symbol

It is true that the coin or the paper money in itself is
of little value, therefore we must learn to get the consciousness of prosperity to back up our handling of the symbol,
so that if the symbol should be taken away or devalued, we
will still be prosperous. When we get to the point where we
can see this thing from the proper viewpoint and work from
the mental level, we can bring all things, including money,
into our life pattern. I am dealing with the subject of money
in this book because to be free in our society we should be
able to handle it. The way to handle it is to confront it and
master it, realizing that in your ability to handle money
you show ability to operate in consciousness. When you

lose your fear of the symbol, then you can master it. Unless you get over your fear and unless you release your false concepts, you will be limited in your thinking and acting in the world of finance.

Remove the idea from your mind that there is a shortage of money. There is no shortage of Substance, therefore no shortage of money. There is plenty of Substance for everyone and it can manifest itself as money as long as money is the symbol of payment for service rendered. As long as you render some service in this universe you will always have money or its equivalent. You need not take money from someone else to get your share. You need but to give to the world, in the form of genuine service, and you will automatically have your share.

Simply to go through the motions of working on the physical level does not insure a good measure of supply in your life, nor does it always indicate a service being rendered. You may be working physically, or at least going through the motions, but be wasting your time. You may be doing something that a machine could do better. You may not be in your right place in the scheme of things. The world does not owe you a living, you owe the world your service. Again, what are you contributing?

Revise Your Concept Regarding Supply

You will have to revise many of your concepts about supply if you want to move into the world of abundance. Let us assume that you are merchandising a product. You decide to go from door to door to sell it. You can call on two people an hour or sixteen people during a working day. Assuming you get in and deliver your sales presentation. You may sell one person out of every seven you approach, so you would be averaging two, maybe three sales per day.

If your profit per sale is only, let us say, $8, this means that you make $16 or $24 a day. Or from $80 to $120 per week. Or from $4,100 to $7,240 per year if you work fifty-two weeks, five days a week. What if you take a few days off for vacationing or have to stop a few days because of illness in the family? Your income drops. With this income you just get by after all expenses and taxes and you have no reserve to draw upon in case of emergency.

Now . . . assume you handle the same product and you hold on to the idea of door-to-door selling. But instead of doing it yourself, you take on distributors who do most of the leg work because they can only work on that level. You are doing them a service by giving them a job. They are serving you and the consumer because they are doing the walking for you and servicing the customer at the same time. You will have to plan for them and also keep them inspired so they will keep busy. You get a percentage of what they make, which isn't as much per sale as you made, but you have several men selling so you have a greater volume of sales. You can buy at better prices and you can use some of your spare time to sell a little also. On your sales, the entire profit is yours.

Say each man who is out selling for you averages $100 per week or $5,200 per year, of which you take 15 percent. If you have ten men earning this amount of money their total earnings is $52,000 a year and your 15 percent comes to $7,800. Add to this the fact that you are buying at less cost because of the volume which is moving, plus profits from your own sales, and you can see the possibility. And, if your product is a worthwhile one, you are servicing more people and rendering a greater service. Conceivably you could take on more salesmen and even handle a product that would still fit the rule of being a real service, but which would allow you a greater percentage of profit.

What have you done? You have given employment to a number of willing workers and you have serviced a greater number of people than you could have done had you kept the door-to-door route for yourself. And back at the plant where they manufacture the product you handle, they will love you for increasing their production and giving more work to the community. Everyone is blessed and there is no reason why you should not be compensated for your ability to work this plan. You have helped a great number of people to help themselves and you have expanded your consciousness to where you get greater satisfaction from living.

You can go on and multiply this process. You can hire a public relations man, you can advertise, take on more distributors, branch out into new markets, come up with innovations. The possibilities are endless and you can go as far as you want to go and be constructive in the process. It is a matter of using creative imagination and of being able to handle larger responsibilities.

Stretch Your Mind

Again, let us be reminded: That which the mind can conceive of as being possible can be realized. It is not a matter of luck, whom you know, proper background, or any of the common statements regarding success. It is a matter of your being able to conceive of your dream as being possible. Everything falls into place as a result of this vision. "The land thou seest, to thee will I give it. Arise, walk through the land in the length of it and in the breadth of it; for I will give it unto thee" (Genesis 13:15, 17).

When you come to this point where you can see the limitless abundance which is yours, you will get over the idea of being envious of the good fortune of other people. There is plenty for you too when you learn to appropriate it . . . when you learn to see how you can do it. Gradually slip behind the scenes to see what is taking place.

No Competition

You can add such zest and a sense of uniqueness to your particular service that even if someone else seems to be offering a similar service there will be room for you too, because your service will appeal to your kind of people. Instead of trying to beat the other fellow out of business, make yourself unbeatable and concentrate on rendering a real service.

Take Stock of Yourself

Erase any concepts that you might have concerning the idea of money being evil or dirty or that it brings disaster in its wake. Money is only a symbol and it is our reaction to it that is important, or in a larger sense, our understanding of it. Money is a simple method of storing service units. Your use of money determines the attitude that others will have about the money that you handle. If you have negative ideas about money you must work with yourself until you are able to resolve them.

Release the idea that it is a crime to have more than your share of money. What is your share? Shall we determine this by the lowest common denominator and gear our personal income to the poorest wage earner? Shall we be content to just get by like 90 percent of the people of our world? Do you believe it is fair to draw an income of $15,000 to $25,000 or even $50,000 to $100,000 a year, or more, while the fellow down the street works his heart out for $4,000 to $7,000 per year? Why not? The same law of prosperity is available to him as it is to you. Do you feel guilty for having more than enough? Resolve these feelings, for they limit your expression. You can handle just as much money as you feel you are worth.

How much are you worth? This does not have to be the measuring rod of your over-all existence but in this sense of money, how much are you worth? Not how much does the bank account show at the moment, but how much can you handle in this world?

Perhaps your service is a good one but you are reluctant to put a price on it. If it isn't worth the price you feel you should have, then why waste your time with it? If it is worth more, why sell yourself short? When you allow others to partake of your services without placing value on them you do them a disservice and it makes it more difficult for you to service others for lack of an honest income. And it destroys your self-respect.

See the One World

I think we often separate the material from the spiritual world. We do this in our own thinking and this is the cause of much conflict and pain, for there is no separation. Many businessmen go to church or support charitable causes and with their families and friends enact the role of the perfect gentleman . . . yet at the office and in the business community they exploit others and use selfish tactics to get ahead. There is no reason for this when you understand the laws of life.

On the other hand, we find people who cling to the idea that it is spiritually elevating to be poor and this concept keeps them in the limiting round of activity that has been theirs for so long. We even find these people resenting others who have more than they have instead of enlarging their own vision to experience their share of good. Resentment will not bring you riches, and pious satisfaction with poverty will not make you any more spiritual.

In the field of religious education, for instance, we find an inner resentment on the part of would-be students if a charge is made for the time involved in receiving the instruction. I have known many sincere teachers in this field who never have been able to see their work expand and flourish because they either accepted the false belief that they were ahead of their time or they allowed themselves to be abused by well-meaning but unknowing men and women.

Invest in Yourself

I will gladly pay a man who can show me how to improve my life pattern and avoid mistakes. Payment in cash is cheap compared to the time I will save in accomplishing my goals. Learn from what others have been able to learn . . . and when you serve others and show them how to live better and on a higher plane, do not feel squeamish about accepting payment. You are not taking from them, you are giving them what money cannot buy. You are really serving them.

I believe we must invest in our future. We should not feel backward about buying books that will help us on our way or in taking classes that will make us more efficient. If you care enough for your future, then do something about it.

Transcending the Appearances

You can train yourself to transcend the idea of "tight money," "recessions" or "depressions." While there may be trends and cycles, there are still opportunities available for those who can see them. Witness the numbers of men who have made great fortunes in so-called "bad times." And others who are able to stand unshaken while the world falls about them. Your world is the result of your concept of it and is not dependent upon what others may think or do. Do not place yourself in someone else's station in life ... find your place and operate from that point, and when you do ... all will be well with you, regardless of conditions at large.

If you remain firm in your understanding of these basic principles you need never fear again, never lack any good thing, anything that is required. If the symbol of supply is removed from view, you can externalize it at will because you know how to do it. We live in an ocean of Mind Substance which is ever changing, according to the impress of the mind of man.

Learn to get the "wealth consciousness." Mix with people who have it. I'm not talking about unnecessary show or flashy appearances, but I am talking about solid wealth. About your awareness of it. Mix with people who have this awareness, not to get their money or property but to attune to that level of consciousness so you can appropriate your own.

Whatever it is you desire to have, you can have by learning to appropriate it. That which you desire to have in your life pattern is either already in existence waiting for you to take it, or it can be brought into manifestation as you visualize it and bring it from the invisible to the visible. Get the idea that supply is all around you and all you have to do is open the door so it can flow into expression in your environment. If you open the door wide enough, a flood-tide will engulf you. After you get into the stream of financial prosperity it becomes easier to remain in it. The important thing is to get it started by rendering a worthwhile service and by adjusting the mental attitude concerning the subject.

You Must Want to Handle the Stuff of This World

If you want to handle money you must want to accumulate it. Remember, desire fulfills itself, so you have to have the desire to see money accumulate before it will begin to do so. You must learn to saturate yourself with the desire for the accumulation and handling of the things of this world so that you have an air of financial stability about you. This is magnetic and will tend to attract desirable situations and opportunities. You must not fear to come into contact with reality on this level of expression. You must be willing to play the game of life according to the rules on this plane of operation.

Plan Your Move

Open yourself to inspirational ideas and plans that will surely form as you have the earnest desire to manifest wealth. Remember, there is plenty of money, but there is a great need for worthwhile projects and sound ventures. Can you map out a sound business venture? One that cannot fail? There are men with money just waiting for you to come along to show them how to put it to good use. So, step number one in this program is to outline a complete plan and work it out in vivid detail. Get it to the point where all you need is the money to launch it and make it a reality. I'll bet that if you will do this, by the time you have it ready you will also know how to raise the money to get it going.

If your plan isn't complete you don't need financing. Why should you have money if you will waste it . . . or if you are not ready to spend it? Get your plan ready . . . carry through with this first step.

Lay it out in detail. If you need to read books which will help you round out your store of knowledge, do so. If you need to get professional advice, do this too. Do whatever you need to do to get your plan in motion. Act as though you cannot fail.

As you go over your plan in detail, perhaps you will see how it can be improved and why you are just as fortunate that you haven't had the money up until now. Be sure to look at your plans objectively and without emotion and sentiment that often go along with a creative idea. When you are sure you are right, then you can be emotional and enthusiastic. Be honest in your evaluation. If your plan is worthwhile, then push through and bring it into manifestation. Don't settle for second best if you can have the very best right from the beginning.

Perhaps you do not have the ability to do everything needed to put your plan into finished form. Then you can contact someone who is an expert in that area and either compensate him for his services or form an alliance with him. Perhaps both of you can do a better job than either one alone. Do not be ashamed to ask for advice. You may not know everything that you should know but you can acquire the knowledge if you are willing to do so.

Besides writing an outline of your project, if possible make a scale model of it so you can see it and feel it. This will make it more real and your subconscious will begin to accept the fact that it is as good as accomplished. If you cannot make a scale model, then have an artist draw a picture of it, or cut pictures from magazines. This takes the outline out of the abstract and starts the process of materialization on this level. The more you can believe, the more magnetic you will be, and this will draw circumstances to you that will have a direct bearing on the fulfillment of your project.

Your Basic Desire Is Important

Whatever you decide to experience, you must experience unless you neutralize or modify the decision. When you arrive at a decision to have a definite experience and you feel this deep down in the core of your being, then forces begin to move in the Ocean of Mind, which is all-pervading, and people who are in tune with your life purpose begin to come into contact with you. You begin to see opportunity which enables you to make definite moves in the right direction.

Most of us desire many things, but only those things we consciously or unconsciously decide to have will come into manifestation. Decisions also motivate us to do what we can to bring our dreams into reality. When you accept the end as a reality, this automatically creates the means for the fulfillment. So, here is another question: Can you imagine what it would be like to have all the money you need, and more?

Work Your Way Up

I had lunch with a friend of mine just a few days before writing this chapter. This man has had a remarkable career in just a few short years. I asked him, "What sums do you think in now, in terms of business dealings?" He thought for a moment and said, "A few years ago I used to think in terms of under $100,000, but now I think in terms of

$1,000,000 and up, with about $3,000,000 being my limit at the moment."

A story in *Business Week* on the dealings of Col. Henry Crown, who controls a multimillion-dollar empire which includes Material Service Corporation and General Dynamics and an interest in the Conrad Hilton Hotel chain, tells of how, in his early schooldays, Col. Crown would "think big" while working with his bookkeeping course. He would add a few zeros to make theoretical deals bigger. His philosophy is, "You have to work just as hard to get a few thousand as $100,000." Really, since we have to be busy at some creative enterprise, why not think in larger terms and be more comfortable?

If you cannot think in large terms you will never be able to talk with other people who do. You will not be in their world at all. Wipe the idea from your mind that it takes psysical effort to make money. You may be active physically but the important thing is imagination. Sometimes a person will say, upon seeing a rich man's son, "I'll bet he never had to work a day in his life." Often the children of rich parents try harder than any other people in order to prove themselves to themselves. You are entitled to all the money you can accept as long as it flows into your life through clear channels and at no one's expense. Energy expended does not mean a thing if it is misdirected.

When you know what you want in life and do only what is required to experience it, you know a great secret. It is this: he functions best who works with nature's law of balanced economy. When you learn to expend energy only for the accomplishment of specific goals you relieve yourself of a lot of waste motion and you accomplish more in a given period of time. Do not waste your time doing things that have no bearing on your goal. Do what you must do, then shift your attention to new areas of operation. All successful men and women are individuals who know where they are going and what they must do to get there.

Communicate with People

Your worthwhile experiences come through the lives of other people, so you must get into communication with them. To receive your supply of desirable experiences you must not only be able to adjust your acceptance level but you must be willing to communicate with people who can act as instruments through which they can flow. This does not mean we are going to use people but it does mean that we are going to be open to the flow of life between people. People cannot help you if they do not know you. You cannot service them if you are not in communication with them. Are you in good communication with other people? Or, do you allow yourself to persist in the belief that people are bad, selfish and mean? Are you afraid of others? Are they afraid of you? Do you give them cause to be suspicious of you? Are you doing everything you can to open the lines of communictation?

The Open Door to Riches

Another basic law is: You must give before you can receive. I'm not speaking of self-denial and wasting time on noble causes. I'm referring to the importance of getting the feel of life flowing through you. When you withhold, it implies you feel there is a shortage in the universe. When you squander, you dramatize your will to fail; but when you learn to truly give, you find that you are a channel for the never-ending flow of goodness, be it in the form of money, love, creative talent or whatever form it takes.

When you give with understanding you connect up with the main supply line, for belief that it is now flowing is the switch that turns on the power in your life. Are you giving to life? You must give, not with the idea that you will receive a reward, but with the full realization that as long as you give in proper measure you will have an inexhaustible storehouse from which to draw.

If you give money to a person or to a cause that is not grounded in sound policy you will waste your money regardless of your good intentions. You do not have to give "conscience money" to buy retribution for your supposed wrong acts of the past. Give where it counts, where it will really do some good.

Giving is not a matter of reckless spending beyond your capacity to earn. Be wise in the management of giving and learn the law of circulation, and you will know what it is to be truly prosperous.

Your own consideration is the measure of your standard of living. If you want to enlarge your concept of your place in life then learn to look at life as do the people who operate on a grand scale. Get into communication with such people. Mingle with them, learn all you can about them. Let them help you if they want to. Do not reject any offer of assistance as long as it does not violate any of your feelings about what is right. You must be great before you can handle greatness.

It Is Your Right to Be Rich

It is your right to be rich. I will step beyond that and say that I believe it is your responsibility to be rich if you want to serve in as great a measure as possible. It is not always necessary to have cash in your possession but you must be able to do the things you want to do. When you can move freely in this world, doing what you feel led to do, regardless of the scope of the project, then you are rich. With riches you can extend your influence and be of greater service to a larger number of people.

Now, let me list a few things that you can do to enable you to break any psychological barriers that you might have that are keeping you from the realization of prosperous living. Practice all of these things until you move into the feeling of wealth.

1. Get used to the feel of money. It is surprising how many people are actually afraid to handle money and use it. Learn to handle it and be sure to rid yourself of all negative feelings concerning it. See it for what it is, a convenient form in which to store your units of service until such time as you desire to exchange it for something else you want. Reach into your pocket now and get a handful of money and count it out. Look at it. Handle it.

2. Get used to thinking in larger terms. Some people feel panic-stricken if they have more than fifty dollars in their pocket. They are afraid they might lose it even though they never have lost money before. It makes them feel uncomfortable. Others, on the other hand, carry several hundred or even several thousand with ease.

3. Practice this: Count out some bills, but instead of counting by ones, fives, tens and twenty-dollar sums, count in one hundred, one thousand, five thousand, ten thousand and twenty-thousand-dollar sums. Get the feel of doing this. There is no particular magic in the process but the experience of doing this will give you an expanded state of consciousness in relationship to money. It will help you establish a mental pattern that will reflect in this world as large sums of money. Do this every day for six months. Do not let anyone see you and do not tell anyone. The idea is to

saturate your consciousness and then reveal to the world through your demonstration of abundance.

4. Some men have found it to their advantage to carry with them a sum of money, say fifty or one hundred dollars, and just have it available without any intention of spending it. This gives them a feeling of being able to spend at will and to pay their way. If they find themselves in a position where they have to pick up the check for lunch or dinner or where they see something they want, they are able to spend without reminding themselves, and thus impressing the subconscious, of their inability. I'm not suggesting a dependence upon the symbol, but any technique that will help a person to operate more freely is helpful.

5. Make it a point to mingle with successful people. Put yourself in contact with situations that approach your ideal. Drive through neighborhoods, move through stores, live on the level that you would, were you the person you envision yourself to be. Your subconscious will "photograph" the surroundings and more and more you will be able to accept these experiences.

6. When you go to sleep at night, do so with the feeling, "I am wealthy." Let it sink into the consciousness. The idea is not to hypnotize yourself, but to awaken the realization that it is true.

7. Refer to the chapters in this book on the technique of creative imagination and practice as described.

Once you get the knack of rendering a service on a modest scale, if you want to feel your way and test your market, then duplicate your service and you will increase your income. Many men start off well but they fail to duplicate their cycle of creative action and they slow down. Set up your business operation so that it will run pretty much on automatic, then turn your attention to expansion and increased efficiency. When you render a service, go all the way. Give yourself to life and life will open the treasure house to you. A man may attract to himself any force in the universe if he will make himself a fit receptacle for it, establish a connection with it, and arrange conditions so that its nature compels it to flow to him.

It naturally follows that as your income increases you will have to learn to manage your money, invest it and use it wisely. A good book that will give many ideas is John Appleman's *How To Increase Your Money Making Power.**

REMEMBER TO PRACTICE:

1. Contemplate the symbol of money and get a real understanding of it.
2. Get rid of the negative concepts and ideas that stand in your way.
3. Get the mental picture of your true worth.
4. Get your plan of action completed.
5. Get into communication with people. Be alive.
6. Practice the techniques as outlined . . . until you get results. You will.
7. Plan to operate in grand style and start from where you are . . . build up to your envisioned level . . . then go beyond.

* Published by Frederick Fell, Inc.

9

CONVERTING IDEAS INTO REALITIES

In keeping with the theme of this book, which is to relate
the subtle things of life to the practical experience of everyday living, I will go into greater detail concerning how
you can convert your ideas into realities. Your ideas have
to be "materialized" or brought into phase with this di-
mension to be real to the senses.

The only thing that keeps many men and women from
experiencing the fulfillment of their dreams is a thin veil
of belief. Here is a story to illustrate the point.

On Lake Tanganyika the natives paddle out from
shore quite a distance and then form their canoes into a
line, facing the shore. They pass wooden poles from canoe
to canoe and start for the shoreline. The water is clear, and
with the sun overhead a shadow is cast down through the
water when the light strikes the surface of the water across

which the pole is held. Underwater, it appears that a dark
sheet has fallen from the water's surface to the bottom. The
fish act as though this shadow wall were impenetrable and
swim away from it as it advances. Soon they are in shallow
water and are easily scooped up into nets. Now, the only
thing keeping these fish from swimming to freedom as the
wall comes nearer and nearer is their impression that the
shadow wall is real and solid.

While we may chuckle at this story, we might also relate it to our own life situation. Many of the walls which
seem to be closing in upon us, driving us to ruin and disaster, have no more reality than the shadow mentioned in
the above incident. We only think they are real and we act
accordingly.

We must, then, learn to discriminate so that we can
perceive the truth about life. We can do this as we learn to
confront life's situations and handle them. We have accepted so many things as having independent reality when
in truth we are more often than not victims of our own
mental creations.

Why do men go through life struggling with poverty,
limitation and disease? Because they create these situations
for themselves by their constant visualization. They make
them real in a personal sense by believing them into manifestation. The way out, then, is to begin to visualize the
desirable things and believe them into manifestation.

Learning Your Lessons in Life

There is no reason for you to remain at a certain
level in your work or activity just because you were born
there or because the circumstances of your environment
seem to have placed you there. Your place in life is where
you feel you can best contribute . . . where you feel free

and creative. A mature person knows that he does not have to harbor the same viewpoint forever, just because he has held it for quite a long time. If you want to change your life, then change your viewpoint concerning life and move on . . . it is that simple.

The worst thing to say is, "Well, here I am. I don't like it but I guess there must be a lesson to learn or I wouldn't be here." The only lesson you have to learn is how to solve your problem. When you realize this you will rise above the present life pattern, if it is holding you down, and you will move into a greater expression. Are you willing to try it?

Think Big and Stand Tall

Here is what T. Russ Hill, outstanding businessman and self-motivator, had to say to a group in his organization early in 1961.

"Set a goal as high as your imagination will let you carry and then strive for that goal every single day of the year. . . . Are you passing by or are you climbing high? The years ahead are loaded . . . the sky is no longer the limit . . . the biggest factory has not been built . . . the tallest skyscraper is still a dream . . . the cures of man's ills are still in the test tube . . . the biggest jobs have not been done in the sales field . . . no product is yet the final word in any given avocation . . . you have not yet dreamed how tall you can be or, in fact, how far you can go."

T. Russ Hill knows how to convert dreams into realities. One of eight children of a country preacher, he worked his way through school and finished at the top of his class in college. He enlisted in the Air Corps during World War I and was commissioned a first lieutenant in eleven months. He became president of his own company at the age of twenty-four. He has been president of four other companies which he largely built. One of these he built from a $187,000 company to a $30,000,000 one in less than fifteen years, with branches in 235 cities and more than 10,000 salesmen in the field. He has also been president of numerous service groups. He was a millionaire by age forty, is the author of twelve books, and is well known in the field of philanthropy. He is considered to be one of the greatest after-dinner speakers in the country.

After you have been stirred to make your move, then you must know how to go about it.

Four Simple Steps to Follow

1. The Idea or Desire.
The ethers are running over with ideas and we seem to tune in to them according to our level of awareness—that is, if we are open-minded. There is nothing wrong with having desire, for we must desire to have experiences before we can move into them. Compulsive desire, or a desire for anything that is inconsistent with our life plan or purpose, will cause us to waste time and energy. But a desire which, if fulfilled, will enrich our life experience and which will bless everyone with whom we come in contact, is good.

2. The Selection and Decision.
This is often the biggest problem. Creative people often have so many ideas that they are at a loss to know which ones to spend time in developing. After you have decided to accept an idea or project and have mapped out a course of action, then make it a part of you by establishing the feeling that it is as good as accomplished. Do this even before you try to think of how it will manifest itself, or through what channels. This is a very important part of

the program. Too often we are reluctant to dream big enough because we fear that we lack the skill or ability to make the dream come true. Do not let this stand in your way . . . begin to feel that your dream is a reality . . . now. Remember, the acceptance of the dream as being fulfilled automatically wills the means for the fulfillment. Begin to feel that your dream is a reality. Now.

What happens when we make a decision? Well, we live in an ocean of Mind-Substance which is constantly being molded, formed and modified according to our mental imaging. When we take a firm stand, we begin to see our world take shape about us to conform to our inner pattern of believing. If we cease to believe constructively, then we must be content to see our world form about us to match our fears and weakest thoughts. We are always proving what we believe. Every hour of every day we are molding and shaping our consciousness by our thoughts, feelings and deep-seated beliefs . . . and our state of consciousness reflects as our experience.

Now, when we remain steady in our convictions, we begin to see situations come into our lives to confirm our believing. We begin to meet people, see opportunity, find talent, money and inner guidance coming to meet us at our level of acceptance in order that our new dream might be materialized.

It is well to remember the impersonal operation of this law. Even when you see the right person, the opportunity, the talent, money or ideas coming into expression, all this is the result of Universal Mind-Substance flowing to meet the need. Do not believe for a moment that these outer reflections are cause . . . they are the effect of the inner mental imagery.

3. The Firm Belief That the Idea Is as Good as Manifested.

You must continue in your belief even before you see evidence that it is so. A well-known industrialist was once asked, "How do you account for the fact that you have amassed so much money and property when in the beginning you had nothing?" The rich man said, "You are wrong in your assumption. When I started out I had everything, and all I did was form it according to my will. Everyone else has the same opportunity." All available substance is here right now. It is a matter of giving it proper form in the appropriate time and space.

You take the raw material and manufacture that which you want to hold forth as your creation. It is that simple. Even when you are creating failure and confusion through disorganized thinking and feeling, you are being creative, only your creation is not in keeping with harmony and perfection. The inner pattern has to be rearranged so it will reflect order and balance. Instead of seeing what you don't want, begin to see what you do want . . . then make it real to the sense of touch, real to this world.

When you are sure you are right, say, "No, thank you," when people who do not share your vision try to change your mind. Keep your own counsel, maintain your inner inspiration and move steadily in the direction you know to be right.

4. See the Desire Fulfilled.

The key to seeing your dream come true is to bring yourself to the point where you can take responsibility for it. This is the crux of the whole matter. If you can take responsibility for the situation you want to bring into manifestation, you will move out and do what you feel you must do to make it appear. You will do what you can do to make your dream a reality. A sense of timing may be in order but you will not wait and pass time because you lack the nerve to move when the time comes.

As you know, most people are the effect of everything that takes place about them. They are easily motivated, manipulated, guided and directed. It is almost as though they wanted others to do their thinking for them. You must be willing to rise above this level of consciousness. You must be willing to respond to life, of course, but you should also be willing to initiate action, to be cause, to get things in motion. Can you take the positive step in the right direction?

You can see as you look about you that the men and women who are balanced and who are doing things in this world are the people who are not afraid to handle the stuff of which the world is made. When you grasp the concept that everything is a manifestation of the same basic Substance, then you lose your fear of handling anything.

Too many people still cling to the idea that to be spiritual they must renounce this world. They still hold to the belief that to be poor is to be rich in the things of the Spirit. In truth, we can operate in grand style and still be spiritually aware. In fact, I believe that the more aware you are, the greater you ought to be as an influence for good.

Synchronize Thoughts, Feelings and Actions

When you decide to make your move, go all the way by synchronizing your thoughts, feelings and actions in the same direction. Put everything you have into your plan. Your posture, your dress, your tone of voice and your mental attitude indicate your true feelings. Just going through the motions is not enough. To think good thoughts is but a step in the right direction . . . you must bring your feelings and your actions in line with your thinking.

Step up to a mirror and look at yourself. Do you like what you see? Is that the image of the successful man or woman looking back at you? Should you do anything to change the picture? If you should, then do it now.

Too many people who think they know some of these laws of life are merely "armchair experts." They sit and hold the right thought but they seldom enter into the game of life. They miss so much joy and depth. They are afraid to get into the swim of things and cannot take advantage of opportunity when it presents itself.

When you really know your right place in life and are firmly anchored in it you will find others coming to you to agree with you. It is really a matter of your self-image. What you believe yourself to be, you see in your world. Others tend to recognize you for what you recognize yourself to be. Do not be shy therefore, about assuming a self-image that will enable you to express freely in this world. Most people are so insecure in their own place in life that they will enjoy seeing your confidence and ability being put into expression. It will give them hope to see you succeed.

Many years ago, after I had studied this material for some time and felt that I knew it well enough to lecture on it, I began to organize public lectures and classes. Imagine my surprise when I found that although I knew my subject and could present it intelligently, I didn't have great success. A friend of mine who had been active in this field for a number of years took me to lunch one day and during our conversation he said, "Roy, your problem is, you know your subject but you don't believe in yourself." That was all it took to push me in the right direction. There is a big difference between the idea and the feeling.

I have noticed that most men in public work seem to be just about as effective in one geographical area as another. I have observed this in my own lecture work, and whether in a large city or a small one, the public response is about equal to my expectation. It is obviously a reflection of my self-image in relationship to others.

Emmet Fox and the Mental Equivalent

In my travels I have talked with many men who knew Emmet Fox, beloved speaker and author of several inspirational books that continue to sell at a rapid rate. Emmet Fox spoke for years in New York City to one of the largest audiences in the world. At one time he drew a crowd of 7,000 to his weekly lectures. He had what is known as a "crowd consciousness." He told his friends an interesting thing about his inner work in relationship to his public ministry and this ability to draw large numbers of men and women.

He used to say that he "carried his audience in his subconscious." Every summer he would recess his talks for a few months and take a vacation. Many of his regulars would go to another church for the summer and remain there as steady members. Dr. Fox found no wrong in this because he felt that each person ought to be in his right place if he was going to experience the fullest in the way of harmony and right action. In the fall, when he resumed his lectures, he always had a full house to speak to, not always the same faces but always a large audience.

It was his practice, so he said, even when he was on his summer vacation, to retire and go to sleep at night with the inner picture of himself standing before vast throngs of people. This was his mental picture that he sustained and it was reflected in his world to such an extent that his ministry is still the talk of the metaphysical world.

Time, Space and Circumstance

It is helpful to know why situations come into manifestation, why they persist in time and why they fade away.
When you understand this you will be able to control your
environment. These rules are to be related to everyday
experience and there is no situation where the rules do not
apply.

Let us look at the law of creation; bringing abstract
ideas into visibility. We do not create something out of
nothing. We seem to create situations as we establish them
in mind and then make them real by moving into them
with feeling. As long as we feed the creation with attention
and energy it will remain in manifestation. When we withdraw our attention and energy it will begin to fall apart.

Say a young man starts out in business. It's a small
business operation in the beginning but it has possibilities.
Now, if this young man runs the business on his own he
will have to be constantly inspired and motivated in order
for the business to run smoothly. Since it is his creation,
it will rise or fall with his efforts. It will grow as large
as he can imagine it to grow or it will fail to the extent
that he begins to believe it can fail. Whether or not it
thrives is up to him. He was able to bring it into manifestation by catching the picture and by bringing it down, in
a practical manner, to the world of the senses, to conform
with this reality. By following through with his creative
work he can expand his operation and make it more stable.
If he has a subconscious "will to fail," even though he has
brought it into form, he will begin to do things to cause it
to fail. He will not communicate with the right people, he
will overextend himself in advertising, he will not keep
proper records, he will do something to throw a hitch into
his otherwise smooth-running operation.

If he can take success, he will do everything on every

level to insure it. Quite often, it is advisable to have two or more persons involved in a business venture because it is doubtful if both of them will make the same mistakes. Then, if one person loses interest for a time, or fails to maintain his enthusiasm, there is still the fact that others can carry the organization. They begin to accept the "image" of the enterprise as being solid and something that will persist through time, and they act accordingly. The more people you can get to believe in the reality of your creation, the more likely it is to remain operational.

In other words, to be successful you must continue the creative process. Many people can create a situation but they cannot keep it going. To keep it going you have to maintain the enthusiasm, the energy and the attention. Any activity will thrive with attention . . . a business, a marriage, any activity at all. When you withdraw your attention from an activity it will wither and fall apart.

Now, many people can create situations and they can hang on to them, but they cannot get rid of them when they want to. The secret of dissolving situations is to redirect the attention into a new channel. Often we find this hard to do because we have an emotional tie-in with our creations. We know we ought to let them go but we cannot do it because we feel a part of us will die as a result. This need not be, and to be in full control of our lives we should be able to let situations go when they no longer serve a useful purpose.

Take a man who begins to merchandise a certain article and it just does not catch on. He should do some research to find out why it is not selling. Perhaps he needs to change the package . . . change his sales approach . . . try a different market . . . even drop the idea and try something else. But no, this man often sticks to his first idea and his project fails. Then he says, "The world isn't ready for what I have to offer," or "I've got a failure pattern," or "I haven't got what it takes."

Let us take two people who go into marriage with their eyes open. After a couple of years they find they are moving in different circles. They don't have much in common. They really do not want the responsibilities of married life. If they could re-create the glow and enthusiasm they had in the beginning they could be happy, but they do not want to do this, so they drift apart. It may well be that their marriage was not the best thing in the first place and they would be better off if they were to come to a parting of the ways. If this is the truth of the matter I see no harm in it. Too many people get involved in situations that they find almost unbearable, then compound the mistake by refusing to clear the matter up.

A man will say, "I made a decision and I'm going to live with it." We all make decisions and from time to time we change our mind or we have new revelations and we see life from a different point of view. When this happens we may feel impelled to modify our previous decisions or even cancel them entirely. There is nothing wrong with making a change once you have new light on the subject. We are always growing, and as we grow it is only logical that we shall see new facets of life. Release the undesirable picture and be done with it. Do not let yourself be dragged down by feelings of guilt and self-pity. If you do not fit into present situations, then change them by changing yourself first. It is a good thing at times to remember the beautiful past, but only the present is real. Enjoy it! The three things to remember are:

1. Creation—You create a situation by practicing the four steps as outlined earlier in this chapter.

2. Persistence—You cause a situation to persist in time by duplicating the creative cycle.

3. Dissolving—You cause a situation to cease to exist in time and space as you take your attention from it and throw it into a new project.

This is the key to handling all of life's problems. When you have a problem, catch a vision of what the solution would be and then bring it into manifestation and you will have no problem. You can be the master if you will only try. The only reason you experience ill health, business failure or domestic friction is that you have nothing you would rather do instead. This may sound harsh, but think about it. What would you rather be doing than what you are presently doing? You must be someone. You must do something. You must have some experience. If you will not project yourself into the foreseeable future and create a place for yourself, then you must be content to live in present situations. If you have a dream of business success, of being healthy and happy, of being happily mated . . . then do something today. Make your move by adjusting your mental attitude. Begin to believe in yourself and move into your heart's desire.

Now, you will need motivation. You may want to read these pages over and over again. You may want to read the stories about how other people were able to move ahead with boldness and break through into the light of glorious self-expression. As you read, you will feel hope surging in your breast. You will come alive. You will feel convinced that you are on the right track, and this is the hardest part of the whole thing . . . you must get this conviction that will not be shaken by temporary setbacks and tempting diversions. You will lay out a program of action and define your goals as to when and where and how much. As you do all of this you will begin to impress this on the subconscious mind. It will become real and this will trigger off a chain of thoughts and ideas that will fit into the

larger picture. And . . . one day you will be there. This
is the formula that never fails. Behind every successful
program these basic laws are to be found.

Practice Revision at Night

At night, just before dropping off to sleep, practice
revising the events of the day. Go over them from the first
moment of awakening to the present moment. See them
as you would have liked them to be. This creates new
tracks in consciousness and helps you to break patterns
which heretofore have held you in check.

If you take emotional problems into the sleep state
you tend to seal them on the subconscious level. When you
release them you prevent the gradual accumulation of pain
and failure and you can then face each day with confidence
and the proper mental attitude. This is important because
the attitude with which you view the world is the window
through which your own life experience comes in to you.

Think About Your Projects

Take a few moments now to think about your projects.
In order for them to materialize you will have to communicate with the right people, for people are channels through
which you receive help. You do not get anything from them
. . . but you receive it through them.

Think, now, what can you do to make your dream a
reality?

You Are Being Reborn

You will surely find that as you alter your outlook
on life you are led to move into new circles. You may feel

impelled to change your place of business. You may change your residence. You may no longer have anything in common with the people you have known up to this point. While it is true that a mere change in acquaintances, or a change in residence, may not alter your level of consciousness or your personal fortune, it may well be that a change in your mental attitude will be followed by a series of changes in your outer life as you receive inner guidance and follow your leading. You will have to do what seems right to you. You may be impressed to alter your style of wearing apparel or your hair style (if you are a woman) or you may be impressed to change your name or the spelling of your name.

We are being reborn constantly. You are not the same person that you were when you began this book. You have already changed in some way as you have altered your decisions about the future and looked at yourself in the light of day. Why bother to condemn yourself or others? Why not live in the moment and plan to move into the future with confidence?

Condense Experience Through Concentration

A philosophical view of life is that plants are energy-binders because they trap energy through the agency of the sun and chlorophyl; animals are space-binders because they can move from point to point in space; and man is a time-binder because he can learn from what others have learned and save himself the time that others used to get the experience. He can use this recorded information, as it applies to himself as a springboard to greater heights. Either through contact with others or by reading about them or their findings, we learn to avoid the mistakes they made and we can take advantage of their successful experiences . . . and relate their findings to our own projects.

Libraries and bookstores are good sources of biographies and autobiographies of men and women who have been successful. When you read their stories, especially if they are in line with your own goals, you can relate their experiences to your own. And you can be inspired, which will in turn trigger off a flood of ideas which can be used to advantage. If you get one good idea from a book it is worth more than the price you paid for it.

I am an avid reader. I buy books, magazines and newspapers and read them when I travel or whenever I have a spare moment. I do not try to accumulate a lot of facts. I seldom take notes. I pick up ideas . . . ideas that I can use in my own work.

I often answer advertisements for free literature describing a book or a course of instruction. I do not always buy, but I want to see how their material is presented. I want to see what is proving successful. I want to know what is going on in this world. I think it is highly advisable to be aware of what is going on in your world, especially in your field of activity. Check on the business operation of others who are in a line similar to yours. Realize there is plenty of room for everyone, but at the same time see where he has streamlined his operation and also see his shortcomings. By doing this you will learn things that will serve you well.

Feeling Is the Secret

A number of years ago while on one of my regular visits to Miami, Florida, a friend invited me to attend a lecture in the high school auditorium during a week night. The meeting was open to the public and the speaker was Jim Jones of the highly successful Abundavita Food Corporation. I had read his book, *If You Can Count to Four,* and had kept up with his activities, and I must say, I was impressed with his rapid rise in the business world. The lecture was well attended and Jim Jones gave a good account of himself on the platform that night. The next day I called him at the Americana Hotel in Miami Beach and talked with him for a few minutes. During our conversation I mentioned that we must have read a lot of the same books and heard many of the same lecturers because our ideas were similar. He quickly remarked, "That's true, but remember, when we take a principle and use it, then it becomes ours." He knew this and it worked for him. When you know it, it will work for you.

Another time, I heard Neville, the popular speaker and author of a number of excellent books on creative imagination, speak before a large audience in the Ebell Theater Building on Wilshire Boulevard, in Los Angeles. After his lecture he invited questions from the audience. One lady asked, "How often should I come to your lectures to get the best results?"

A lesser man would have told her to come to every session from now on. But Neville said, "Come as long as it takes you to understand what I am saying, then go out and use it to make your life a wonderful experience."

Here is what I would do upon hearing a good speaker present his ideas; I would sink into a reverie and feel that it was I who was doing the talking. I would alter my point of view so that I felt I was doing what he was doing. This feeling enables me to bridge the gap from being the listener to being the speaker. We have to start somewhere. We start from where we are and move, in our imagination, to where we want to be.

If you do not know how it feels to be the person you want to be, then you must identify with someone who is doing what you want to do. You are not to lose your individuality but you are to gain the viewpoint as represented by the other person. The only difference between the person who sees success and the person who sees only failure is the point of view. It is that simple.

There are men and women with less intelligence, less schooling, less experience than you, and yet they have a better position, more influence and happiness. Why? Because they have accepted their position in life and acceptance is the key. For remember, the acceptance of the dream fulfilled automatically wills the means for the fulfillment.

Now relax and contemplate this for a while . . . until you understand the full import of it.

As Within, So Without

Your world is effect. Your mental imagery is cause. Therefore, always work from the world of cause. When you do this you work from behind the scenes, from the projection booth, as it were, and you can master the pictures that appear about you as your world.

Here is a story of a most unusual man. Dr. Masaharu Taniguchi of Tokyo, Japan, heads a religious movement by the name of Siecho-No-Ie, or "The Home of Infinite Life, Wisdom and Abundance." Almost thirty years ago, this organization was just an idea in Dr. Taniguchi's mind. He was working as a translator for a business firm and he was moved by a feeling that he should initiate a movement that would show people how to live in line with natural law.

He thought it all out and figured that if he saved a portion of his income for a while he would be able to start publishing a small magazine that would take the message to the people. So he began to save his money. After he had saved it for a while and was about ready to publish the first issue of his proposed magazine, a thief broke into his home and made off with his savings. Again Dr. Taniguchi began to set aside a portion of his income . . . and again it was taken from him.

Like anyone else, he wondered why this happened to him when he was consciously doing his best to be helpful. As he sat in the silence, contemplating this situation, he seemed to hear a voice from within the depths of his mind. Of course it was the Truth making itself known. The voice seemed to say, "Rise now, don't you know the world is only the shadow of the mind and that the source of all supply is within you?" He was inspired and made contact with the printer immediately. Soon his magazine was under way . . . and today he edits not one, but six magazines a month —five of them in Japanese and one in English. His books have sold into the millions and his followers have been estimated at over ten million. It all began when he looked for guidance and then followed the inspiration that came to him.

Whenever you are troubled, sit quietly and remember, "The world is the shadow of the mind." And you too will move ahead with confidence and make your mark. You can go as high as you can see and higher . . . you can do as much as you can believe for yourself . . . and more.

You Are the Point in Space

Take time each day and relax so that you can attune yourself to the universal power. When you do this, you get in line with it and this power becomes your power. You cannot move it into your idea of how it should operate, but you can move yourself into harmony with it. It is easy to get confused when you identify with restless and purpose-

less people. We tend to take on the nature of our environment and if we mingle with people who have no plan or
purpose in life we begin to think and act the way they do.
It cannot be otherwise.

Your environment is important. Remind yourself that
you have a right to be successful and happy. By a steady
process of straight thinking you can remove any belief to
the contrary. If mental pictures of men who are failures
float before your inner vision, drop the pictures and say,
"It may appear to be true for these people but it is due to
their lack of understanding. It is not a universal law. It
need not be true for me." When fears of the past haunt
you, release them and remember that as a free soul you
are operating from this moment and from this point in
space, and all power is yours because you are in tune with
universal power. When you realize this, what can possibly
stand in your way? Remove any thought or feeling that
stands between you and your fondest dream. Strike it out.
Remember, it is nothing but a shadow and has no reality.

Multiply Your Efforts

As one person you are limited in what you can do in
this life if you depend upon your own efforts alone. You
can be in only one place at a time and you are obviously
limited by the number of hours available to you in a day.
But you can change this if you are willing to change your
mental attitude. I know of a man who was told by his
business manager that if he made twenty calls a day he
could depend on at least one sale. If he made forty calls
a day he could count on making two sales, and so on. This
was average for men selling his particular product. The
salesman was appalled by this information. The manager
was speaking from experience but his word didn't have to

be law. The salesman went into the silence and the idea dawned on him, "Why couldn't I just reverse this idea and instead of making twenty calls to get one sale, make one call and get the equivalent of twenty sales?" He geared his mind in this direction and went to work. Of course, he didn't turn the tables completely around the first day, or the second or the third. But after a while he was actually getting the equivalent of twenty sales for every call he made, either through increased orders or through referrals.

It is really a matter of our concept of life. You know of many people who just manage to scrape by. You know of others who always manage to have a surplus. What is the difference? Have you ever wondered? If you will examine these situations you will find that behind the appearance there is a concept established in the minds of the persons which, for them, is what life ought to be.

Do not be ashamed to accept help from others when they freely offer it. You will arrive much faster if you harness the energy of many people who are going in the same direction as you. Accept all the constructive advice you can get. Accept the boost upward by people who are in a position of influence. Realize that money, rightly used, can help you accomplish more in a shorter period of time. Money is energy in convenient form and it can be channeled with great and far-reaching results. A man with good ideas and a million dollars can get more done, and faster, than can the man with good ideas but no money. The man with money can even hire the talents of others. If you have good ideas you ought to be able to get in line with money as long as you remember that the secret of directing great volumes of energy or money is that you must work with, not against, universal law.

If you can organize and inspire a group of men to do something constructive then you are multiplying your efforts. You are using your influence and intelligence. Regardless of what you are doing, you can live better by using these basic rules. If you are a housewife you can do your work more efficiently and in less time if you concentrate on it. Then you can use your free time to expand your awareness and do things you have always wanted to do.

We have come to the place in our progress where we can turn much of our work over to machines, and now the challenge is to do something with the free time. This means that man is freed from much of the routine drudgery and can now explore new areas of mind and consciousness which is the next logical step in the unfolding of the human race.

REMEMBER TO PRACTICE:

1. Move your ideas from the abstract to the concrete.
2. Understand the four simple steps of converting ideas to realities.
3. Practice the mirror technique.
4. Synchronize your thoughts, feelings and actions.
5. Get a firm grip on the law of creation, preservation and the dissolving of situations.
6. Be a time-binder, learn from others.
7. Live without strain.
8. Live from the realm of "cause."
9. Multiply your efforts.

10

UNVEILED MYSTERIES

A mystery is something hidden, secret or unknown. Life holds many mysteries for us until we awaken to the point where we see clearly. The immortal Emerson wrote, "Our eyes are holden that we cannot see the things that stare us in the face, until the hour arrives when the mind is ripened; then we behold them, and the time when we saw them not is like a dream."

You have had experiences like that. You have searched for hidden meanings and finally seen that for which you had looked so hard. And when you saw it you said, "Why didn't I see it before?" In truth, everything is available to us but we have to bring our inner vision to a point where we can see it, where we can accept it. So many men and women have been wandering down the highways and byways of life, confused and disappointed, looking for the way out . . . when suddenly it dawned and from that moment they began to move . . . and their entire life became a new and wonderful experience.

It does not matter who you are or where you want to go in life, when you catch the vision of who you really are and what it is you can do, and do well, you will move into a world as far removed from your present world as night from day.

Always remind yourself that life is a game. The world is the playing field and there are certain rules for playing this game. There must be rules so there can be order and purpose. Man sets the rules so that he can conduct himself about something stable. Without rules, without order, the average man is unstable and insecure. He must have something to give him direction and purpose. This is basic.

Now, our mental attitude is very important in relationship to our playing the game of life. If you are going to live with people you will have to conform to a degree, with their ideas of what life is all about. You may see beyond their vision, but in order to work in harmony you will have to fit into the race idea of what life is designed for. You will have to be objective . . . be sincere . . . and see things in proper order.

A number of years ago I was talking with one of the leaders in the self-help field and as we talked he said, "You are a serious young man, aren't you?" I agreed that I was and he said, "You should learn how to be sincere without being overly serious."

At times when we are overly serious we lose our good sense and become wrapped up in the world of effects to such an extent that we are lost.

Life Wants to Fulfill Itself

This is a good thing to remember . . . Life wants to fulfill Itself. When you are able to remove the bars of resistance you will find that situations flow into place to confirm your idea of what life should be. Maybe you inwardly know this but you cannot bring yourself to give up the old way of life; the old way of thinking, feeling and acting. Since man experiences what he feels he should experience, it stands to reason that he must alter his state of being if he wants to alter his experience. Our task is to remove the obstructing factors so that Life can fulfill Itself.

To have any experience . . . to do anything worthwhile . . . you must be someone. Everything in your life issues forth from your state of beingness. What you are is the key to the whole thing. You cannot do anything or have any command over your environment unless you can assume responsibility for your actions. Lift up your vision, and all the things of the world that you can see—opportunity, prosperity, happiness, health, good fortune—you can have, for the exalted vision enables you to see that which is already available.

Going Ahead in Feeling

Every human experience is preceded by a psychological assumption. Haven't you ever wanted to experience anything with a passion? Haven't you ever longed for a certain feeling of fulfillment? Your constant imaging of it brings it into your presence. Successful people do not know the difference between the state of imagination and the state of reality when they begin to move creatively. They have learned to bring their dreams effortlessly into manifestation by accepting them as real. They picture their dreams . . . they feel them into existence. They know that if they can sense anything as real, even though it is not real to the eyes of others, they will force it to appear.

We all use this principle from time to time. We have all "felt" ourselves into a state of ill health. We find people who "feel" themselves into radiant health and prosperity, and we find others who do the same thing to produce loneliness and lovelessness. All people use the principle but very few understand it. And even among those who understand it, few employ wisdom in the use of it. Most people are slaves to wandering thoughts and feelings. This is why their world is so chaotic. The secret of transforming the world is to learn to discipline and direct the thoughts and feelings and thus predetermine the life experiences.

A Powerful Technique

Here is one of the most effective methods of bringing your dream into manifestation. When you have defined your goal and you are sure it is what you want, sit down and with pen and paper or typewriter write a scene that would imply that your dream is a reality. You needn't be skilled in writing, just do the best you can, with feeling. Put yourself in the proper role and live it to the fullest. Bring in emotion, speech and action. When you do this, you begin to bring your dream out of the realm of abstract ideas and it takes on a body. You make it more and more real.

Do you know how important it is for you to speak constructively? Do you know how important it is for you to think and feel properly? Then, use this technique of writing yourself into your goal and run your thoughts, feelings and everything you have into the picture so that you are true to your ideal. There is no magic about this . . . it is merely a technique to help you flow your attention in the right direction.

If you are skilled in the use of creative imagination you will not need this method but be sure that your reluctance to use it stems from the fact that you do not need it, rather from a subconscious resistance to change. Many seemingly logical excuses have their basis in a subconscious fear of success. Be honest with yourself.

Beliefs Are Stronger than Wants

It is all right to say you want a certain experience, but no matter what you say, if you subconsciously believe you will never get it, you never will. There is no getting around the law. It is exact. This means we can always depend upon it. It means that once we learn to operate according to the rules of the game, we are free forever.

A belief is a sustained mental image. It is what you know to be true, regardless of what you see about you. And the thing you know to be true is what comes true for you. This is why it is so important to associate with men and women who are confident so that you can "pick up" their feelings and build a sustained mental image of self-confidence. The surface feelings and whims have little power to do anything, but the deep-seated feelings can produce marvelous things.

You will know that you really believe when you are serene. Peace, joy and inner contentment indicate the acceptance of your place in life as being a reality. When you gain experience, it is easier to believe than it is to doubt. Believing, like doubting, is largely a habit. Drop the notion that life must be one succession of painful experiences.

You are worthy of wonderful things, and when you can make this a law on the inner level of feeling you will see it unfold in your life.

Superconscious Awareness Is Superior to Subconscious Conditioning

When you are fully aware, you see life as it really is, but when you are conditioned, you see only through a small opening. A person who is conditioned believes that only his view of life is real, whereas one who is fully aware knows that several viewpoints exist. You must be big enough to see every conceivable point of view in order to be free. To attach yourself to a little view that seems like truth and cling to it is bondage of the worst kind.

We all know of people who have invited confusion by trying to convince themselves that sickness and poverty did not exist . . . yet they saw it at every turn. The proper attitude is this: it is possible for people to experience sickness and poverty but it is also possible for them to change their inner picturing and experience health and prosperity. Nothing is permanent and even the most spiritually blinded person will eventually awaken.

You do not have to protect yourself from negative or evil thoughts or situations. All you have to do is move steadily in the direction of your perfect world. In the last chapter of this book I will give definite methods for seeing things in relationship to perfection.

Self-Motivation

I do not know of a single successful man or woman who does not need to be motivated at some time or another.

It isn't always easy to move steadily in the right direction, for even the most successful people have periods of stagnation. When you feel down and need some motivation, read a book or listen to an inspirational lecture. Do this until you feel your enthusiasm begin to mount and then get busy at your plans so that you see firm results . . . and this will give you confidence.

Many businessmen keep inspirational books handy in a desk drawer or brief case. When they feel the need of a pick-me-up they read a few paragraphs or a few pages until they begin to glow, then they get busy. The sales of self-motivation books have boomed over the past several years, which proves that there is a definite market for books that inspire, instruct and motivate.

So great is this response to self-motivation material that a recording firm has been established which specializes in records based on best-selling inspirational books. In Waco, Texas, Paul J. Meyer has built his organization, Success Motivation Institute, into the largest business of its kind in the world. He arranges with publishers and authors to condense their books, then puts them on long-playing records which are distributed by a sales force across the country and in foreign lands.

Paul J. Meyer is himself a product of his own believing. He became a millionaire before he was twenty-seven years of age, by selling insurance. Then he turned his talents to the area where he feels most at home, in teaching others how to make the most of themselves. He claims the secret of his success is "crystallized thinking," which involves setting down your goal, backing it with a burning desire, maintaining the vision, then paying the price by turning all of your energy and talent in the direction of the goal.

Another Example of What Inspiration Can Do

Everyone who reads this book is surely aware of the ministry of Oral Roberts. In his sermons and writings, Mr. Roberts tells of the experiences that marked a turning point in his life. The following story is just one of many.

One night, many years ago, while speaking in Amarillo, Texas, to the vast throng which had gathered in his giant tent cathedral, a storm came up, and in the wind that accompanied it the tent was knocked down and destroyed. It was a miracle that no one was hurt. The next day Oral Roberts walked about the grounds and viewed the wreckage that had been his tent. This had been a very important piece of his equipment, for it made possible the huge meetings that drew at times over ten thousand seeking souls. He was hurt and disappointed. He didn't know what to do. He had put everything into his ministry up to this point and now it looked as though he was stopped.

The newspapers had carried the story and soon letters and telegrams began to pour in from all parts of the nation. One telegram was handed to him while he was still lost in this feeling of despair . . . and when he read it he began to come alive. A friend who heard of his loss had chosen a telegram to express his thoughts on the matter. It contained just seven words in the body of the message. It read, "Brother Roberts, You Can't Go Under For Going Over."

It was the title of one of the sermons that Oral Roberts had preached so many times. It had to do with man's faith. This message inspired him. He caught the vision of a new and larger tent and a new and larger ministry. And . . . he made his move in consciousness to secure what was needed and he went ahead in a wonderful way. It could have been the end of his ministry but he was motivated into constructive action and moved on to greater things.

Follow Your Highest Intuition

While no one can deny the value of good and wise advisers, there invariably comes a time when we must come to the point where we get our guidance directly from the source. We must learn to operate intuitionally. Intuition is direct knowing. It is always right. In the beginning we may get intuitive feelings confused with subconscious whims, but with practice we can know the difference. When you begin to recognize your intuitive guidance and follow it, you are growing up. You are maturing.

There is nothing wrong with making a mistake now and then. This merely shows that you are progressing. Most successful people have failed at one time or another but we usually hear only of their successes and not their failures. Gradually, as you continue along, your failures will become fewer and fewer and your successes will increase. Do not let minor failures hold you back. Consider them opportunities to grow, to expand, to overcome. There will come a time when you are larger than any situation that you might confront. Then you will be the master.

Awareness Is Power

When you are aware, you have power. You can see all sides to every question. You know, which is better than speculating. When you are aware, you come alive . . . you notice things about you. You avoid mistakes . . . you see opportunity . . . you are automatically considerate of the feelings of others . . . you have a perfect memory . . . you can read at a rapid rate and retain what you read. Yes, when you are aware, you have power.

How shall you increase your awareness? By taking an interest in life. By confronting situations. By looking directly at what life has to offer. By removing the fear that keeps you from coming into contact with people and situations. By being willing to accept life on all levels. Can you do it? Think about it. Try it.

Have you ever noticed how many people are unaware? They say, "I can't seem to understand." They walk as though in a dream. When they get off a bus they stand on the sidewalk, right in front of the others who are getting off. When they cross the street they just amble along, oblivious of the motorist who is trying to check his speeding automobile. When you talk with them they are only partially aware of what you have to say. They are not really living. Most of their attention is scattered out through time and space. They live almost totally as the effect of their environment.

How aware can you be? How much can you know? Do you think it is wrong to know too much? To see too much? If so, why?

When you are aware of this world you can have a long-range view of life. You can build for the future by making the foundation solid. In this way you have a base from which to work and over a period of time the effect is quite striking.

Have a Point of Contact

We have mentioned the importance of being able to identify with an ideal—someone who is an example of what you want to be like. To the extent that you can do this, can you rise out of your present concept of self. Some people go beyond the idea of a human ideal and grasp the concept of the Infinite Invisible. They feel that this Power is guiding every step of the way to the degree that they are able to open themselves to it. Of course, we all have a concept of God or Infinite Mind. The late Carl Jung wrote that man harbors a concept of God that is large enough to meet his need and when his needs increase, he creates a larger concept. How big is your concept of the Infinite? Do you believe in a tribal God who has jurisdiction over a certain area of the planet or the solar system, or do you believe in a Cosmic Presence, so large that It includes everything, even the distant stars?

Whatever your concept of the Infinite—as long as it remains a concept, and it is probably just that if you can still think about it—it is a point of contact for you so that you can raise yourself up to its level . . . in order to see beyond.

I do not believe it is right to pray for success at the expense of another person. If you pray, I would suggest that your prayer be that your eyes might be opened to see opportunity, make the right contact, meet the right person. I have known of salesmen who could pray to make a sale and then go out and do it. This can be sorcery if it is not properly handled. If we use the power of will to control another, then we are misusing the power. If we use the power of mind to find the right person, then we are doing it correctly. It is all right to pray or visualize that the right people are coming into our life, so we can serve them with our product . . . but we must not pray or visualize specific individuals as buying our wares. In the first instance we are being open for guidance and in the second instance we are controlling the will of another.

Many successful men claim they have been guided to make proper business moves when they opened themselves to the "Presence." The feeling that this Infinite Intelligence is working its way in their affairs enables them to relax and helps them to extend intuitively beyond the limits of ordinary sense consciousness and grasp subtle truths. One man I know calls this Presence his "silent partner" and attributes his success to the fact that when he has been able to rest his mind in the assurance of the Unseen Power, he has been guided every step of the way. This is due to the fact that, as we have been saying, tension blocks intuitive insight. Relaxation and perfect faith opens the door to it.

The veil between ordinary living and outstanding success is very thin. Often, all we have to do is take an idea and work with it until it catches on. A case in point is the story told concerning Robert Collier, author of *Secret of the Ages* and *Riches Within Your Reach.*

Robert Collier had made a name for himself in the business world by writing sales letters for firms selling products by mail. He had a knack of writing that was sincere and went straight to the heart. He began to toy with the idea of putting out a set of books that would explain his system of philosophy, but like many of us, for a long time he just carried the idea around in his head.

Then, lightning struck! He got an idea for a sales circular that might sell such a book. It was only natural that he should conceive of the circular before writing the books, because writing direct-mail circulars was his business. He wrote the circular and tried it on ten different lists, a thousand sales letters to each list. The returns were incredible . . . they were as high as 9 percent from lists that were new. He worked day and night to get the books ready and, as soon as they were prepared, he arranged for a mailing of a million circulars, followed shortly after with a second million.

Within six months after the books were ready he had received more than a million dollars' worth of orders for them—all in response to his mailings. So successful was he that he had to take on an associate to help with the mailing department . . . and true to his philosophy, the right man came along, with money and experience, to fit into the job.

The Robert Collier books continue to sell in large numbers, and the business is now looked after by Gordon Collier, son of the founder. On a recent lecture trip to New York City I met Gordon Collier, who told me that the business was booming and that he had taken in several new titles besides the standard Collier publications.

We must have persistence if we know we are right. Sometimes it works out that we hit the top right away. Other times we have to work through seemingly insurmountable obstacles. The man who persists is the man who succeeds. So, when you are sure you are right, forge ahead.

When I was a teen-age boy on a farm in Ohio I used to subscribe to a number of physical culture magazines and I can recall reading about Jack Lalanne, then of Oakland, California. Jack Lalanne had a gym there and was attracting wide attention with his feats of physical endurance. He had a burning desire to spread the gospel of physical fitness and was always pushing to the front with his message. He had some setbacks, to be sure, but through it all he persisted, and now his name is a household word as he is viewed by millions every day on his half-hour television show. But he didn't stop there; he continued to expand until now he is reaching out into other countries with his work.

Its easy to quit when the going gets rough but this is the time to try adjusting the mental attitude . . . and when you learn to do it, you will learn to come out on top. It never fails. A strong vision cannot be held in check . . . it must work out.

A Man of Destiny

Back in 1920, a young man came to this country from India. His name was Swami Yogananda (later elevated to Swami Yogananda Paramhansa) and he had a mission in life. He came to bring the ancient science of yoga to the West. He did not come to convert Americans to a new religious belief; he came to offer basic laws of living. The first few years he spent quietly in Boston with friends —then he made his move. He got financial backing and launched a transcontinental tour of the major cities of the United States. He would book the largest lecture halls, cover the town with posters weeks in advance, run large ads in the newspapers, get the influential citizens of the community to lend their endorsement and then come to town.

The huge halls were filled to capacity for nights in a row as he electrified his audiences with a verbal description of what they could do and how much they could know if they would only believe in themselves and practice some form of mental discipline. He settled in Los Angeles, California, and that is where I met him in 1949. By this time he had built a large and flourishing organization, trained thousands of students and prepared dozens of teachers to carry on the work. My early years following high school were spent with him and he introduced me to the wonderful inner worlds of Mind and Spirit.

So great was his impact that his books continue to sell, translated into more than twelve languages and advertised in such national magazines as *Time, Newsweek, Saturday Review* and many of the large Sunday papers.

He had a dream . . . he was imbued with a mission; and
his enthusiasm, coupled with his ability to adapt to the
times and use modern advertising methods, put it over.
Life held no mystery for him.

An indication that he has done his job well is evident
in that almost every major book publisher carries at least
one title on the subject of yoga in his catalogue. People
everywhere are awakening to the facts of life and are grasp-
ing the science of life which knows no barriers.

Mind Mysteries

Few people today are unaware of at least some
powers of the human mind. Or, perhaps should I say, the
powers of the soul filtering through the mental apparatus.
A Gallup Poll investigation, taken recently, revealed that
20 percent of the American people admitted they had experienced some form of mystical experience. During this
time they felt a great release from old life patterns, a sense
of unity with Universal Mind and in many cases a complete
readjustment of habit patterns. If you think you are alone
in exploring the unknown, just consider that books dealing
with mental science sell into the hundreds of thousands of
volumes. Look over the dust jackets of the current best
selling self-help books and see how many big name executives as well as top people in the entertainment field endorse
these ideas.

No one has ever climbed from the bottom to the top of
the success ladder without consciously or unconsciously
using these methods. This is something worth remembering.
You may like to think you are an exception but you are not.
The sooner you can make your adjustment with life the
better off you will be. Make yourself aware of what is going
on in this field.

Do you know that responsible men are working with the idea of using mental telepathy as a means of communication between earth and space ships? Do you know that research is being done concerning how the mind may influence matter? These things are no longer a matter of speculation, but we need more work before we can bring these abilities under control.

Do you know that man has to break many of his concepts regarding life on this planet if he is to face the very real possibility of intelligent life on other planets? A conservative estimate puts the number of bodies in space that are similar to the planet earth at one hundred million.

I believe that man must learn to be aware of his real nature if he is to keep his sanity in outer space where the familiar orientation points do not exist. We are being forced to extend ourselves in this space age.

It has been proven under strict test conditions that when the conscious mind tension is removed, the soul of man can reach out to distant points in space and tap the reservoir of all knowledge. It is not necessary for you to be hypnotized to be able to do this. You can do it through controlled reverie, as you have learned from the earlier part of this book dealing with creative imagination.

Dr. Joseph Murphy, minister of the large Divine Science Church which meets regularly in the Ebell Theater in Los Angeles, tells of the following incident. A number of years ago he was on the first leg of an overseas trip. The plane on which he traveled went via the polar route and stopped in Greenland for a few hours. In a mountain cabin where he was served coffee, he was approached by a man who said, "I used to listen to you in Los Angeles. Will you go and see my brother in Copenhagen?" He added, "I knew you were coming. I saw you in a dream and I knew also you could explain matters to my brother and straighten things out between us."

Dr. Murphy did meet this man's brother and was able, through discussion and prayer, to clear up the matter between the two. How did the man see Dr. Murphy in his dream? Is it possible that we can attune to the subtle things when we are free of the conscious mind resistance? I believe so, and many others do too.

As I write I have just returned from a lecture tour that took me to five cities in the southeastern United States. When in Miami and St. Petersburg, Florida, I spent a number of hours on late-night radio, being interviewed in the former city by Larry Glick of WINZ and in the latter city by Bill David of WLCY. On both shows, after we had opened with discussion, we accepted phone calls from listeners and I answered their questions on the air concerning ESP, positive thinking, dreams, visions, self-motivation and related subjects. Just about every person who called could relate a story that seemed to bear out the fact that extrasensory experiences are more common than we imagine. Many could tell of their dreams of a member in the family having passed from the body or of occasions when they were in telepathic communication with friends at a distance, such communications being borne out in later contacts by letter or telephone.

Attracting Things

We can learn to attract our heart's desires. We mustn't try too hard, remembering that we can do best that which we do most easily. Most of us can work this way in some instances but not in all. For example, I have always had a "book consciousness." I like books and I attract them; even if I don't buy them, they are given to me or they just turn up. Not long ago I decided that I wanted a copy of Mark Twain's book on Christian Science. I didn't want it because of his outspoken criticism, I wanted it for some of the data it contained. So, I held the idea in my mind and let it go at that. A few weeks later I was speaking in Dayton, Ohio, and while there I stopped in at a store where they stocked my books. In our conversation I happened to mention to the sales clerk that I was looking for Mark Twain's book. She told me that even if they had a copy of this particular book it would probably be in a set and they wouldn't want to break a set. After browsing for a while I started for the door, and was stopped short as the sales clerk called to me. Turning back, I was confronted by her as she held a well-used volume of the book I wanted. She told me, "I was just going through a box of books that came in this morning and found this one title by Mark Twain among the lot by different authors." I bought it.

This happens so many times that it cannot be chance. Others have told me of similar experiences, either in connection with books, pieces of art work, furniture or any hard-to-come-by articles. We all know men and women who find it impossible to attract anything, but there are others who attract everything . . . money . . . opportunity . . . friends and companions. That which you can accept easily, you can have . . . and in abundance. Hence the saying, "The rich get richer and the poor get poorer." The solution is not to take from the rich and give to the poor. The solution is to teach the poor in spirit how to have great faith and get rid of fear and resentment and the idea of poverty. Then they will attract all that they need for a complete life expression. If you have a dominant consciousness you will find things clinging to you and the world will press treasures into your hands. Every man can work the law . . . every man can apply himself and alter his circumstances.

At times we hear people say, "You can't change circumstances." I do not care where you live, in what country or under what form of government . . . if you want to expand your consciousness and live a richer, fuller life, you can. We are working with scientific methods. Remind yourself that if one person has done the impossible, you too can do it.

You may find others who do not agree with you. Do they share your vision? If not, then pay no attention . . . as long as you are on the right track. Norman Vincent Peale has been criticized for his "positive thinking" approach, yet while many of his critics remain unknown, he continues to reach millions through his articles, books, columns and sermons. Almost every breakthrough in the field of mental science has been greeted by negative remarks.

Thoughts Through Space

Harold Sherman, author of inspirational books and recognized as a world authority on ESP, co-authored a book with Sir Hubert Wilkins entitled *Thoughts Through Space*. In this book they related their experiences in sending communications mentally from the Arctic regions to New York City. Sir Hubert went to the Arctic to search for some lost flyers and before he left he agreed to try to communicate with Mr. Sherman at prearranged times.

The results were astounding. The telepathic thoughts and messages received by Harold Sherman registered in his consciousness so distinctly that he received them more frequently and more accurately than the messages sent by radio to *The New York Times*. This was one of the most carefully controlled experiments of this kind ever attempted, with daily records being kept by Dr. Gardner Murphy of Columbia University.

Anyone can learn to receive impressions if they will learn to relax and open themselves with an attitude of expectancy. When you want to know of the thoughts and feelings of another person, whether that person is in the next room or thousands of miles away, just sit down and relax . . . wipe the mind clear of all thought . . . look inward to the reflecting screen of the mind . . . and soon, as you identify with the person on the feeling level, you will begin to get impressions, ideas and images relating to that person. It will take practice but it can be done.

I know of spiritual leaders who keep themselves "attuned" to their students in this way and can thus guide them with proper instruction from time to time. Again, may I say that distance is no barrier to this practice. Time and space are relative considerations and need not stand in the way of our communicating with others.

Just as you can receive impressions, you can also project your thoughts and feelings by willing another person to know of your presence. Just concentrate on another person, with your eyes closed. Visualize them as though they were in your presence. Feel it to be so. If they are receptive and if you have successfully visualized . . . they will feel your thoughts and feelings concerning them. You are where your attention is, regardless of where the body appears to be.

While some researchers feel that it is the mind that sends and receives thoughts and impulses, I feel that it is really the soul or the unit of awareness, which is our real identity, and that the mind is the filter through which awareness flows. Hence, the more we can relax the conscious mind and just be aware, the more effective we tend to be in our practice.

ESP Not a Gift but a Natural Ability

One of the questions most often asked is whether or not extrasensory ability is a gift. The answer is that it is merely

an ability that we should awaken and use. In many people
it remains dormant because they are reluctant to be aware
to the point where it can manifest itself. They are afraid
of what they might see if they were telepathic. They wonder
if they have the right to know the thoughts and feelings of
others and if they might not be made aware of a lot of
unnecessary material.

In the first place, when we become sufficiently aware to
know the thoughts and feelings of other people, we should
also be mature enough to know that a human being is capable of thinking and feeling almost anything at some time
or another. We should also be sophisticated enough to be
discreet and keep many things to ourselves without judgment of others.

In the second place we need not be concerned with being
bothered by a lot of negative or random thoughts that are
floating about, because our own mental attitude will guaran-
tee that we attune only to the level of our desire. Reluctance
to be aware is one of the prime reasons for our inability
to operate as freely as we should.

Everyone knows of the work of Dr. Rhine of Duke University. He has done much to make ESP research respect-
able through his writings and regular reports. Dr. Andrija
Paharich, with his work in ESP and the investigation of
the Sacred Mushrooms and related material, has also contributed to the public acceptance of this subject. When the
television series, "Alcoa Presents," put on a weekly show
dramatizing incidents of a psychic nature, the entire country
responded favorably.

ESP Demonstrations on Radio and TV

A friend of mine, Dr. Gilbert N. Holloway, has appeared on hundreds of hours of radio and TV programing

over the past few years. Dr. Holloway travels quite a bit
and lectures to interested persons on his philosophy of life.
When he is in a city to speak he offers to appear on the
local radio and TV shows. So successful is he that it is not
unusual for him to be on as many as five radio stations and
three TV stations within a two-week period in one city.

Thousands saw him on the Mike Wallace show and it is
hard to estimate the total number who have observed this
talented man demonstrate his ESP ability in this way over
a number of independent stations. A remarkable thing
about his appearances is that he not only discusses the subject with skill and a high degree of intelligence but takes
telephone calls from the listening audience and without
ever having seen them, tells them things about themselves
right on the air or on camera, as the case may be. Allowing
for his forceful personality, allowing for his occasional
generalizations, he is usually right on so many points of a
personal nature that there is no doubt that he does tune in
to the person with whom he is talking. He claims his secret
is to be in a state of positive receptivity.

Living in the Present and Foreseeable Future

Happy people live fully in the present while they plan
for a succession of enjoyable experience in the near future.
With short-range projects and long-range goals they have
something to give them a feeling of direction and purpose.
This assures peace of mind and a certain sense of fulfillment. People who are overly concerned about the present,
who try constantly to patch it up and hold the line, tend
to become neurotic. They magnify their problems instead
of doing something constructive about them. We are happy
and mentally stable to the degree that we can get ourselves
adjusted in time in relationship to our goals. The failure

lives in the memory of "what could have been" but the successful person lives in the vision of "what life can be."

You can surely learn from past experiences, but it is a mistake to live in the past. A lady came to me for counsel. She had a common problem ... she was out of work and didn't know where to turn. She felt that she should be able to use her talent rather than work for someone else but she didn't know how to get started. We talked awhile and I learned that she had once owned her own fashion design shop and had even promoted her own shows to get her designs before the public. I suggested she use her talents for promotion and sell her services to someone who might have need of them. She caught the idea and before long was representing a man in the investment business. She was able to use her talent and apply it to a present time situation.

One of the hardest things to learn is to abandon ourselves to our new idea of life. Too often we try to hold on to the past, which is only natural if we are unaccustomed to operating in the higher level of mental activity. But to succeed, we have to make a break with the past. Sometimes it is painful ... other times it comes easily.

Dr. Donald Curtis, in his books, *Your Thoughts Can Change Your Life* and *Human Problems and How to Solve Them,* tells of his experiences in changing from a career of acting in the movies and television to a career as a minister of Science of Mind. Every step of the way was not always clear and he had to constantly apply himself in order to move ahead ... but he did it, and now he holds regular meetings in the Lindy Theater in Los Angeles, is on radio daily and his books reach out to other seeking souls. Dr. Curtis knows from experience that the inner pattern must first be established if the outer world is to reflect order and right proportion.

The Working of the Perfect Plan

We often change from one path to another and it seems that everything we have ever done was a part of the picture as it fits into the present pattern. I know my varied background, even the experiences that I wouldn't choose to repeat, have caused me to be more philosophical and have given me greater depth and understanding.

The important thing is to have a long-range goal and then let the little things in life emerge as a part of this over-all picture. As you practice living in depth you will find that you break into ever larger and larger worlds of self-expression as you resolve to fathom the truth of life.

REMEMBER TO PRACTICE:

1. Remind yourself that life is a game, so learn the rules.
2. Project your feelings, remembering that psychological assumptions precede physical experiences.
3. Remember that beliefs are stronger than wants.
4. Know the value of self-motivation to action.
5. Awareness is power . . . therefore, be aware.
6. Have a point of contact with the Infinite.
7. Dare to explore the mysteries of the mind.
8. Draw life's treasures to you through applied mental magnetism.
9. Live in the present . . . plan the future.

11

QUESTIONS AND ANSWERS

In order to make this material practical to the reader, I have included a number of frequently asked questions with answers to them that I think will be helpful.

Q. Isn't it dangerous to encourage a man to think big when he is obviously limited by his natural talents?

A. The purpose of this book is not to build a sense of uneasiness in people so that they are constantly striving for the unobtainable things in life. Its purpose is, however, to encourage them to extend themselves so as to live to their fullest potential. We must be reasonable in our plans for the future, but we must also remember that most people use only a fraction of their true ability. Anyone, within the framework of his own thinking, can greatly improve his lot in life and come more closely allied with the creative power.

Q. What if I practice the technique of creative imagination, for instance, and nothing happens; that is, conditions remain as they are?

A. If you practice the technique of creative imagination with intense feeling and live in the dream and make there-here, and then-now, you will most definitely move into a new experience. Conditions may remain as they are but you will move into new conditions. The reason for failure in moving into the dream is that the feeling has not been established as to the reality of the new state and so the attention remains on present situations. The solution is to cling to the vivid feeling of the new and desired life experience and ignore the present if it does not conform to it.

Q. Isn't this an attitude of wearing rose-colored glasses or of ignoring the obvious facts of life?

A. Only if you live in a fantasy world and gloss over the surface conditions which remain as they are. The proof must be in the demonstration or materialization of a new and desired situation. If we do not bring the new experience into existence, then we can be accused of living in a fantasy world. The proof must be forthcoming.

A painter must get his work before the public . . . a businessman must communicate with his market and keep a flow of merchandise or services going . . . a writer must be published . . . a lover must be loved . . . and so on.

Q. What if I apply the technique of creative imagination and when the desire materializes it is less than I pictured it to be . . . where do I go from there?

A. Why accept anything less than perfection? The choice is always ours to make . . . whether we will take second- or third-rate experiences or whether we will go first class. It has to do with our ability to accept the best that life has to offer. Often we do not feel worthy of the best and so we take anything that we can get. The solution is to alter the inner acceptance level.

Q. Isn't there the possibility of being controlled or manipulated by others who are aware of this technique? Or, on the other hand, do I have the right to declare what I want, especially if it involves other people?

A. A few moments' reflection will bear out the fact that in this world we either impress others with our will or we are impressed by others to do their will. We are always falling under the spell of other people. We have suggestions thrown at us from every direction, from billboards, the printed page, radio and television, even in our most intimate conversations with friends and associates. It is impossible not to be influenced in some manner. The trick is to accept only the suggestions that are in line with our own goals and plans for the future.

The main factor that gives us a degree of control as to how much material we accept without thinking is our ability to be aware. The more aware you are, the more perceptive, the less you are liable to be influenced by suggestion, verbal or telepathic. Remember the basic rule . . . man can only experience that which he believes possible. If you believe it is possible that men can be controlled, and especially if you indulge in the effort to control men's minds, you are liable to be controlled also.

' In your creative work it is best to work impersonally. That is, imagine a situation as though it were now in existence . . . and let the right people come into it with you . . . as they have a need for this experience. Never use your ability to visualize to control other people or make them do your bidding.

I am often asked to give advice as to how one might cause a specific person to pay attention to him, to be a friend or companion. The best way to handle this situation is to feel yourself to be so strong and self-sufficient that you automatically draw the right people to you. To force

others to share our life is to violate the law of non-inter-
ference. Never do to others what you would not want them
to do to you. This advice is not based on the idea of cause
and effect but rather on the law of correspondences. That is,
you can experience only what you can believe to be true
for others. So instead of being obsessed with getting . . .
try to see others as recipients of good fortune. As you believe it to be possible for them, so it will be possible for
you, according to your belief.

Q. Is it right for man to desire experiences other
than those he now has? Shouldn't he try to be content with
his lot?

A. Man, by nature, is not content and this makes him
different from any other created thing. Coupled with this
discontent, he has his wonderful imagination by which he
can project himself into situations other than those he has
currently experienced. As long as we do not force others to
bend to our will then we do not violate any moral code. We
should realize that our present station in life is the result
of all we have ever imagined possible. Therefore, we are
responsible for the present and we can also take responsibility for the future. The idea that our lot in life is given
to us by another intelligence is rationalization for not
changing for the better . . . it indicates a lack of courage
to confront the real challenge of life, that of plumbing its
depths. The Infinite Creative Power has no personal will
for man. Therefore man can write his own ticket. The door
to unlimited self-expression is always open and the choice
is ours and ours alone to make.

Q. Do these methods always work, or is it a matter
of hit-and-miss?

A. We always reveal to the world that which we believe to be true. Our personal world is the reflection of our
inner imagery. The fact that our present situation is a per-

fect reflection of deep-seated beliefs is proof that it is an exact law with which we are working. If it works at all it works all the time . . . and in every situation. Our task is to learn to live according to the laws of life. The laws never deviate.

Q. How do I know what is best for me?

A. This is one of the most frequent questions. We are often afraid to make a decision for fear it will be the wrong one. Remember that if you make no decisions you must coast along. If you do not try, you will have no experience other than the routine ones. You learn as you try to live according to the laws of life. It is perfectly all right to modify plans once they are put into motion, if later insight reveals a better way. One sure way to know whether or not you are on the right track is to seek inner guidance as outlined in this book.

Q. As I plan my future, what about my responsibilities to others?

A. If there are other people involved in your personal world who would be affected if you changed your present pattern, then plan to have them taken care of also. The wonderful thing about this method of operation is that no one is left out . . . everyone benefits.

It is unfortunate that so many people drift through life under the false belief that they must sacrifice themselves to others. You can always see to it that members of your family are taken care of properly. Don't think for a minute that they won't survive if you make an adjustment in their routine. Human beings are pretty tough creatures and have a marvelous ability to adapt.

The main thing is to work for the best interests of all concerned. At times you will find some people in your environment who will resent the fact that you are becoming more creative. They will express a desire for you to be content with your lot so they will not have to undergo any change. If their wishes are unwarranted and emanate from a small point of view, disregard them. Do not be malicious or try to teach others a lesson, however.

Q. According to some philosophies, desire is a binding force and keeps a person involved in this world. Can we desire and still be free?

A. Man can have no experience without desire. The only kind of desire that binds is compulsive desire, which is inconsistent with present time goals and purposes. This, of course, leads to conflict. Man is continually moving forward into his psychological assumptions. This is how he unfolds into greater and greater states of awareness. We start out without desire, almost in a state of apathy. Then we pass through the various stages of desire and fulfillment, becoming more aware as we go, until we reach the desireless state of serenity. Serenity is at the opposite end of the line from apathy.

Q. Aren't these principles rather basic and isn't it true that there are deeper things in the realm of the occult and metaphysical sciences?

A. It is true that there are more complex systems set forth in many metaphysical books and teachings. Yet, in my personal experiences, after several years in the study of all phases of the occult sciences, I still find that the basic rules as set down in this book are rules of action which are invaluable for people who want to express fully in this world.

There are, unfortunately, literally thousands of men and women in all walks of life who have studied the prescribed lessons in occultism for years and who are enslaved by the beliefs of cause and effect and the idea of limitation.

It is easy to become fascinated by the glamour of the occult teachings and the promises offered by sincere teachers. All too often our studies in this direction tend to lead us away from the very real business of living . . . which is supposed to be what the inner teachings are all about. Inner teachings are helpful to the extent that we can relate them to everyday experience. We are living now. This is the only time there is.

Q.   Should a person be religious or spiritual to derive benefit from these teachings?

A.   Now, a spiritual person, to my way of thinking, differs from a religious person. I feel that a spiritual person is one who is consciously aware of the creative power and works with it. He may or may not have any rigid religious concepts. Spirituality, it seems to me, is allied with creativity.

Q.   Is there any danger of going "off the deep end" through these practices?

A.   As long as you relate the practices as outlined in this book with reality on this plane, you will be kept in line with practical experiences. We are not to build dream castles . . . we are to be conscious instruments for constructing a better world.

Q.   Must we be prepared to sacrifice to gain?

A.   At times we have to make a choice but I wouldn't call it a sacrifice. The idea of sacrifice is due to our thinking in terms of limitations. We live in a universe of abundance. The idea is, of course, to discipline the mind and feelings and to keep the mental cobwebs out of the way. One of the noblest challenges is to keep free of the negative concepts that seem to float around.

Q.   What is the cause of nervousness and tension which sometimes appear when one is working on a project which seems to be important?

A.   When we attempt to move into a new psychological level which is unnatural for us, according to the past experience, we do not always feel comfortable about it. Therefore, we show signs of apprehension and unsteadiness. This is an indication that we are not yet established firmly in the state of being that we are reaching for. We can overcome these symptoms by steady application of the techniques until we get the feeling of naturalness . . . also by endeavoring to synchronize our thoughts, feelings and actions in the direction of our goal. One will confirm the other.

Also, we can insure a sound physical body by attending to the matter of proper rest, diet and recreation. This will be a good foundation upon which to build and will prevent negative subconscious patterns from being stirred up.

Q. Is it dangerous to practice meditation or go into the silence as you suggest? I have heard many views concerning this.

A. The people who talk about the "dangers" of going into the silence are, for the most part, people who are not even willing to explore the idea of meditation. They find a certain security in standing by, finding reasons why they and others should not seek to improve themselves. The important thing is to work from a balanced viewpoint and relate every inner experience to the everyday experience of living. In this way there will be natural unfoldment.

Q. What is the best way to control the mind?

A. The best way to control the mind is to give it something to do. This is why people who are involved with goals are the most content . . . they have their mental activity channeled into constructive work. Begin to affirm that you can control the mind, that you can control the feelings, that you can get involved in a purposeful activity. This is the first step. As for controlling the mind in meditation or the creative silence, refer to any one of a number of methods suggested in the chapter on this subject.

Q. When we sit for guidance as you suggest, is it another "intelligence" that gives the guidance, or just what is it?

A. I do not suggest that we depend upon other "intelligences" to tell us what to do. In the first place, much of this sort of thing is purely fantasy . . . and secondly, it is far better for us to realize that we can clear the mind and receive insight into our affairs as a consequence. When we learn to do this we are free to open to the truth of life at any time we so desire. We should avoid any tendency to shirk responsibility.

Q. In your chapter on money, you deal with a subject that many people are reluctant even to think about. Don't you think that our present world condition is due partially to the fact that there is so much emphasis placed on money and not enough placed on the spiritual values?

A. I believe that many people do go overboard on the money angle, yet they also seek power, which is an attribute of the soul. They need to learn to look behind the symbol and catch the picture of what money really is . . . merely a convenient form of storing up units of service. The real challenge is, What shall we do with our money? How shall we spend it? How shall we be good stewards and channel it intelligently?

I feel that a balance must be struck. There are thousands of men and women who claim to seek the truth of life, yet they are barely existing . . . they are under a strain. Others desire to share their wisdom with interested persons yet lack the funds to promote their work. Money can be used to great advantage. It can back up ideas and make them real in this world. The idea is to transform men's minds so that they will have proper motives. This will solve the problem. I encourage the average person, not to desire a fortune if this is not a basic desire, but to desire an abundance, so that the strain of living can be lifted.

Q. How will I know when I have found my right place in life?

A. You will know when you have a sense of fulfillment, a sense of being a part of the whole. Also, when you see door after door opening to you and situations forming to confirm your ideas. When you are in your right place you will know harmony and peace. This is a dynamic peace, however, and is not a passive state of rest.

Q. Just what is ESP?

A. The initials ESP stand for extrasensory perception. This means that when you are aware of something, such as the thoughts of others, an event that has taken place at a distance or when you become aware of subtle trends taking place in human affairs, even when you have no evidence to support your feelings, you are using ESP. You are really using your intuition . . . your ability to know directly. Most people can improve upon this ability by being willing to know about life. Many people choose not to know because they think it is normal not to know. Really it is abnormal not to know and is an indication of a fear to face life.

ESP ability is not a gift, although some people who are able to relax seem to be able to demonstrate it more readily than others. When someone in your family begins to manifest ESP ability, take it just as naturally as though it was the most normal thing in the world. Do not make a fuss over it, especially when it manifests in children, for this will only point out that they are different. Since we do not like to be different we often stop using certain abilities in order to conform to what most people feel to be a normal behavior pattern. The trouble is, most normal people, while being able to adjust to their lot in life, seldom do anything worthwhile . . . they just live out their existence, content to let others do their thinking and knowing for them.

Q. Just how much responsibility do I have to visualize world conditions as being harmonious? Also, in this rapidly changing world how can one sustain any enthusiasm when the future is so uncertain?

A. Since this world is our home at present, I feel that we have the responsibility for seeing that it is an orderly place in which to live. One must, of course, study the world situation in order to know where best to throw his support . . . but it always helps to look ahead and be optimistic concerning the future of the human race. The future is certain. We are in the beginning of a new world order . . . which will culminate in a golden age. The challenge is not how to avoid destruction, but how to make the transition in an orderly fashion. A race of people who are creative and who understand the laws of life will help in this orderly transition.

Q. What would you say is the most important thing to remember from reading this book?

A. I believe that the most important thing to remember is that our world is the reflection of our believing. With the understanding that the world conforms to our expectations, we have the key to controlling our destiny.

12

THE WORLD IS YOURS

This chapter should be related to all others in this book. In it you will find the key to solving the mysteries of life. I have presented many viewpoints, techniques, methods and ideas . . . in order to reach you where you happened to be as you read the material. One thing you have learned thus far, at least in theory, is that your world is largely what you make it. In truth, the world is yours.

The present is the result of past decisions. If you made your present situation, you are responsible. You can either keep it the way it is, modify it or change it. You created it in the first place, therefore you can re-create it.

Man's problem is, he forgets that he created his situation and he accepts it as being superior to himself . . . thus he is bound by circumstances. One of the reasons he feels this to be true is that he does not feel comfortable about his being here. Most people are conditioned to feel that it is wrong to be happy and successful . . . to experience pleasure. Hence, they feel unworthy of even desiring to alter their lot in life if it is not ideal.

The first step, then, is to awaken to the realization that you are a conscious instrument for the molding of the substance of this world. Without you and others like you the earth would be void of anything except nature's creations. Your imagination is needed that the world might take your pattern and form. You are responsible . . . therefore you have every right to handle the substance of this world . . . all of it.

We have already found out how we limit ourselves by accepting ideas of smallness and inadequacy . . . we have already found out that we have a truly great creative ability if we are willing to use it. But, perhaps we are confused, befuddled by the world of appearances in which we live. You may recall that we have been stressing the fact that the world is not an illusion . . . but our concept of it constitutes the illusion. The world is real . . . but it has no independent reality. Science confirms this point . . . that all matter is reducible to energy. Every form—chairs, cars, desks, trees, people—is energy appearing as the form that we see. Understanding the nature of things as basic substance (energy), we see how we might, by introducing new causes on the mental level, be instrumental in altering the appearance of any form. It takes some clear thinking but it can be done, and this is the theme of this chapter.

Mastering Time

Time is not law. It need not bind you. The truly aware man acts now. Anything that he wants to do, he can do now . . . in his imagination . . . which is the first step in the process. "But," you say, "what about the facts?"

By facts you refer to circumstances. But circumstances

are the result of planned imagining; and since they are results or effects, they can be altered. When you move into the realization of "now" then you overcome the time gap. Outer circumstances are reflections of inner movements in mind. The time it takes for you to move from the appearance of sickness to the reality of health will be the time it takes for you to fully accept health as the reality. The time it takes for you to move from the appearance of poverty to the realization of prosperity will be the time it takes for you to accept prosperity as the reality . . . as the law of your life.

When you understand the nature of this world you will automatically express fulfillment in every area of your life. There is no room for lack or limitation in the illumined mind. An illumined mind is one that is devoid of darkness or ignorance.

An illumined mind is clear. How clear is your mind? Are you allowing it to be cluttered up with negative thinking and erroneous ideas? If you are, then it is reflecting in your environment, for this is the law. When you can clear the mind you can experience harmony in your world. When you have a clear mind you can move through time in an orderly fashion . . . you can schedule your activities and keep to your schedule.

When you learn to do this you can also learn to handle yourself in space. You must be able to operate in time and space if you are to be free.

The Grand Purpose of Existence

Everyone sooner or later contemplates it. I think it is a good idea to contemplate why we are here and where we are going. It gives us a larger perspective and it forces us to be honest with ourselves as we relate present actions and desires with the long-term goal. When we are honest we build on a stronger foundation. We are naturally ethical in our conduct. We automatically treat others in the best way possible.

It is not only good business to be honest, but when we are, we tend to attract others who are honest because we tend to attract our own kind. This honesty will make life far more meaningful and give it a depth that will be extremely satisfying.

The purpose of life seems to be that we might eventually attain knowledge of self. In the process we are confronted with the solving of problems that come up as a result of our lack of understanding. That we can devise solutions to problems is in itself a miracle and to be able to carry through and solve them is to draw nearer to the source of life.

Too many people move through their weeks, months and years without really knowing the joy that comes from conscious recognition of what the whole thing is all about. Think . . . look back over the golden moments when you dared to really live . . . I mean when you reached out and took life to the full. There is no reason why this joy in living cannot be a constant experience. We are immortal souls, most of us concede this point . . . at least we intuitively feel it to be so. Shall we wait for some other time and place to come into the full realization of this thing? This, of course, is a decision that each must make and on it hinges much of what can be done with the material in this book.

With a real zest for life comes the ability to abandon oneself to the great experience of growing . . . learning . . . achieving. Without this willingness to live, all the efforts will be hollow and without real feeling. This is why I stress the importance of enjoying life.

We grow old and die when we begin to accept the "facts" of life. When we psychologically decide that there

is nothing worth living for . . . no longer any reason for
being. This psychological death always precedes physical
death. When the time comes, as it will, when you can accept life, then death will no longer claim you . . . for death
is a shutting down of awareness . . . a giving up . . . a
blanking out.

You can "create time" by having something for which
to live . . . by projecting yourself into the future as you
conjure up worthwhile plans and goals. Remember, your
experience emanates from you, so that, regardless of your
physical age, you are still the creator . . . you still call
the shots.

What Is the Basic Motivation?

What drives us on? We may feel that it is the desire
to impress others . . . to be secure . . . to prove our worth.
But really, the basic drive, though it may be disguised as
lust for power, for knowledge, for name or fame . . . is
the urge of the soul to know itself. As the soul unfolds in
conscious awareness, this unfoldment is reflected in the
external life pattern . . . as man breaks through into new
areas of thought . . . novel dimensions of time and space
. . . thrilling phases of motion and feeling. Every man
has moments when he knows beyond a shadow of doubt
that he is greater than even he dare dream and that his future is undeniably glorious. At these times he is propelled
onward to his sure destiny.

The Master Consciousness

The state of awareness that we come into when we
find release from all the negative and erroneous concepts
I call the "Master Consciousness." For it is from this level

of awareness . . . this consciousness of being . . . that we can survey our world as it really is . . . without the distortions and blind areas causing a clouding of the facts.

It is from this level of awareness that we are able to move with masterful purpose and handle any and every situation that we might choose to confront. It is from this vantage point that we can see through the appearances as they seem to be and observe the ready solution to every problem . . . the answer to every question.

A person who is problem-centered can never work his way out of a problem. The best thing he can do is exchange one problem for another. To solve a problem you must come to a point in awareness where you are problem-free. It is a matter of shifting the viewpoint. It takes a bit of practice but it is a knack more than anything else.

In order to confront situations in the light of the Master Consciousness you will have to be able to start with the seeming situation and, in your mind's eye, see the solution. Then you will have to contemplate the solution until it is the reality. This process we call "Translation."

The word "Translation" means to "bear from one place to another." One version that we find in the dictionary states, "to remove into heaven." This is interesting in the light of our present work, for as we are able to come into the right relationship with life we experience heaven on earth, literally. We don't go anywhere . . . we merely make an adjustment within ourselves.

Steps in Translation

There are four simple steps in the process of "Translating" appearances into what they should be according to the principle of order.

1. Realize the nature of this world as Consciousness

(energy at this level) and that everything you behold is a manifestation of it.

2. Confront the problem . . . see it clearly. This simple practice will often cause it to solve itself as you see through it. You must be able to confront the problem if you are to see through it and bring forth the solution.

3. Contemplate the truth of the matter from the view-point of the first step . . . that is, realize that the situation is Consciousness appearing as the situation. There is no other Reality. You are dealing with basic substance now. It may not be appearing (molded) according to harmony but it is still basically the same substance. Since substance is easily remolded, you can solve any problem.

4. Establish yourself in the vision of the solution . . . see the solution and contemplate it as being real with such intensity that it becomes real. Since what you contemplate becomes real to you, when you contemplate the solution, it manifests . . . and the problem is no more. This is "Translation."

Now, let us work in a few practical situations to get the feel of the idea. I am assuming that you will be able to confront the situations as they appear to be . . . then contemplate the ideal as I set it forth regarding:

Health—Health is the automatic effect of my realization of the wholeness of Consciousness. Since body is Consciousness appearing as form according to my concept of it, when I know the truth about Consciousness being perfect, I must have a perfectly formed body. This means that I am in good communication with my body on every level, down to the smallest particle, and my body is in harmony with my world. Though I do what I am led to do in matters of diet and exercise, it all springs forth from my consciousness of wholeness as being the law of my life. My knowing the truth about the nature of the body is cause, the perfect body which is now manifesting is effect. Since I live in the constant recognition of wholeness, my body always reflects health and normal function.

Home—Consciousness is formed according to my acceptance of it. Since Consciousness is the only Reality, it is everywhere present. As I am always in my "right place" I always enjoy a suitable dwelling place. I am never homeless because I understand the nature of Consciousness appearing to meet my need. There is never any time lag, for I live in the present and know fulfillment at each instant. This truth also applies to clothing, food, money and anything else that I may appear to require. Everything is always provided and in full measure.

Money—Money is but the outward symbol, one of many such symbols, of my awareness of Consciousness being what it is. Since Consciousness externalizes and takes form to meet my level of desire, I have plenty of money at all times. I am led irresistibly into creative expression because it is my nature to be involved with life. I relax mentally and abandon myself to this Truth.

Teaching—Teacher or Belief—Consciousness is manifesting as this world; therefore, there is no teaching, no teacher and no unchanging belief. I always meet the teaching or the teacher, which is Consciousness appearing **as,** according to my need and at the time when I am ready to take the next step to the ultimate fulfillment. I retain such beliefs as give me a stable outlook on life, but I easily drop them when new insight affords a clearer perception of Truth.

Companionship—I am self-satisfied and content because I am secure in the realization of my place in life. I am complete. Whatever is required to confirm this picture . . . husband, wife, friend . . . comes into the pattern in a natural and wonderful way. This feeling of self-sufficiency is cause . . . the appearance of the appropriate companions is the sure effect.

Place in Life—My world conforms to my inner knowing; therefore, I am always in my right place in my understanding. I synchronize my feelings, thoughts and actions to confirm this. Thus I am integrated and in tune with the Universal Pattern. I never lack any good experience but my fulfillment is always presenting itself to me and no one is hurt or slighted as a result. Everyone I contact is blessed . . . for this is the law of Consciousness fulfilling itself.

Wealth—Since I fully understand the nature of Consciousness, which is everywhere present . . . never divided . . . diminished or portioned off . . . I have the wealth consciousness. My awareness expands beyond this physical body until I realize the world as my larger body. With this realization I can and do operate on any scale, transcending the confining concepts of size. I realize that Consciousness is everywhere present and lends itself to be formed and shaped. I shape it willingly according to my highest intuitive guidance. I am beyond the concept of getting anything from life, for I see now that it is a matter of forming the ever-available Substance.

Education—I know that true education means to be aware of Life being what it is. It is not a matter of becoming . . . it is a matter of being. All knowledge is . . . for Truth is. All my efforts to read, to study, to learn, simply stir up the inner knowing. Thus I can know anything and I can and am appropriate to every situation.

Time—I know that my concept of time is an acquired one and that it need not contain me. Time is not law. In Truth I live in the moment . . . I do not age . . . do not become bored . . . never wait for things to happen. I am fully aware now. All the Love there is . . . all the Peace there is . . . all the Truth there is . . . is available now and I claim it.

Identity—I am a soul . . . a unit of awareness . . . I exist . . . I am aware but I am not touched by that which I observe . . . for I see it in the proper perspective. I can move in the relative concepts of space and time without being limited by the concepts. I am free of guilt, regret, sense of failure or loss. With the full knowledge that I am the dreamer of the dream of life I project desires and yet remain free of the projection. I have full control . . . I can create, sustain a creation and dissolve it at will. I live easily from the viewpoint of the "Master Consciousness."

Mind—My mind is the filter through which my awareness flows. The subconscious layer of mind receives and retains the images with which I impress it in order that I might create according to the law of this level. The conscious level is a perfect computor, easily assessing present time data and comparing it with past experience and future probability to arrive at the right and logical conclusions. The superconscious level perfectly reflects the light of Truth. My mind is illumined . . . it is free of heaviness, distortions and erroneous concepts. The mind easily rests so that I might perceive the Truth of Life.

Life—Life is Consciousness acting upon itself. It has no beginning and no ending. It moves from motiveless necessity. As I attune to this grand activity I lose the ideas of duality . . . success vs. failure, pleasure vs. pain, sickness vs. health . . . I am aware of Life being what it is— I am serene.

It is obvious that you will have to contemplate these subjects and do the best you can with your inner work. The more you practice, the more the light will dawn. I do not think it wise for anyone to think that they must gradually work up to living from the "Master Consciousness." It is better to assume that it can be done and then do the best you can, than to settle for less. You can do more than you think you can . . . so try to extend yourself a little . . . and you will be more than pleased with the results.

In time you will want to get your own insight into the various areas that we touched upon in this chapter. Your own insight will determine your lot in life and this is the important thing. Not what the authorities say, not what others say, but what you say . . . will be the important thing for you.

These attempts to "Translate" the appearance world to the way it can be are not attempts at autosuggestion. The idea is to awaken . . . to know the truth . . . and this is only done consciously and with full awareness of the process. You can improvise your own "Translations" to suit your conditions. You might want to use the following one if you are a businessman.

Business—Business is an activity in mind . . . it is not subject to patterns of success and failure . . . political trends, weather conditions or geographical location. Human mind is an individualization of Infinite Mind, therefore since Infinite Mind is self-contained . . . so my business, being an activity in mind, is self-contained. I see opportunity at every turn. I rejoice in the business success of others, with the full knowledge that there is an abundance of all good things and everyone is in his right place. Right action is a law unto my life . . . therefore my business prospers.

These methods lead to an expansive viewpoint as we come into a larger understanding of what we are about.

You will find your own way through life, which is as it should be. I am sure that many of the views set forth in this book will help you to help yourself. I have been helped in the writing of it as I have searched to grasp the subtle principles of living the full life.

Day by day, strive to live closer to the Source. Arrange your time so that you can relax, plan, visualize and explore the creative silence. Work your plans . . . get into motion . . . with the right mental attitude.

You are bound to succeed. This is the truth.

I am knowing this truth about you—now.